ILLINOIS 15-HOUR APPLIED REAL ESTATE PRINCIPLES COURSE

AN INTERACTIVE PRACTICUM FOR BROKERS

1ST EDITION

PERFORMANCE
PROGRAMS
COMPANY

STEPHEN METTLING
KSENIYA KORNEVA

Material in this book is not intended to represent legal advice and should not be so construed. Readers should consult legal counsel for advice regarding points of law.

© 2021 by Performance Programs Company
6810 190th Street East, Bradenton, FL 34211
info@performanceprogramscompany.com
www.performanceprogramscompany.com

ISBN: 978-0915777693

Illinois 15-Hour Applied Real Estate Principles Course

Table of Contents

ABOUT THE AUTHORS

For nearly fifty years, Stephen Mettling has been actively engaged in real estate education. Beginning with Dearborn in 1972, then called Real Estate Education Company, Mr. Mettling managed the company's textbook division and author acquisitions. Subsequently he built up the company's real estate school division which eventually became the country's largest real estate, insurance and securities school network in the country. In 1978, Mr. Mettling founded Performance Programs Company, a custom training program publishing and development company specializing in commercial, industrial, and corporate real estate. Over time, Performance Programs Company narrowed its focus to real estate textbook and exam prep publishing. Currently the Company's texts and prelicense resources are used in hundreds of schools in over 48 states. As of 2021, Mr. Mettling has authored over 100 textbooks, real estate programs and exam prep manuals.

Kseniya Korneva is a licensed REALTOR® in Tampa, Florida with a passion for writing and editing. She graduated with a Civil Engineering degree from Clemson University and fell in love with real estate shortly after. Coming from a long line of academics, her love for education runs deep. Kseniya was first introduced to the world of publishing after writing her own ebook in 2019 and realized she wanted to dive deeper. In her free time, she loves to write about personal finance and real estate on her blog (www.TheMoneyMinimalists.com).

KEY CONTRIBUTOR

Sue Miranda-Rosensteel was the founder and President of Miranda Real Estate School in Chicago, a company she grew into one of the largest privately-owned schools in Illinois. Sue has served as Director of Real Estate Education and Senior Manager of Real Estate Curriculum and Instruction for other top leading schools. She currently volunteers her time to serve as a Director in the Association of Illinois Real Estate Educators (AIREE) and a Director/Secretary in the Real Estate Educators Association (REEA) and was recently accepted as a new committee member on the ARELLO board.

15 Hour – Illinois Applied Real Estate Principles Course

Course Overview

The content of this course covers the IDPFR-specified topics for the 15 Hour – Applied Real Estate Principles Course (AREP) as prescribed in The Real Estate License Act of 2000.

Our AREP course contains six chapters. Each chapter begins with an informative text narrative summarizing key points of required content. Subsequently, participants will be given interactive quiz questions and a variety of interactive case study demonstrations, "what if" case studies, and situational case study examples. Students will be required to participate by answering problem-solving questions and situations.

The overarching purpose of the 15-hour Applied Real Estate Principles course is to expose students to more real-life applications of Illinois real estate principles and laws, including:

- how to list and sell properties
- how to comply with agency and disclosure requirements
- how to gear your practice to comply with anti-discrimination laws
- how to work with sales contract provisions and escrow funds
- how to value and price properties

Finally, the last chapter summarizes other key job-related duties and obligations such as teams, compensation, advertising, and a review of activities requiring licensure.

Chapter Learning Objectives and Time Estimate

Chapter 1 – The Listing and Selling Process

Learning Objectives: When the student has completed this chapter he or she will be able to:

- Highlight the components of residential prospecting strategy.
- Summarize the key steps in planning and executing a listing presentation
- Identify the purpose and prevailing types of listing agreements
- Summarize the four benchmarks in the listing process
- Describe the key activities that take place prior to closing and the broker's responsibilities during this period
- Discuss the impact of electronic communications on residential brokerage, including MLS, emails, social media and smartphones
- Summarize essential advertising regulations framing one's brokerage practice
- Identify the principal elements and financial entries in the seller's net sheet.
- Calculate a buyer's estimated closing costs

Course Time: 4 Hrs.

===

Chapter 2 - Chapter 2: Agency and Disclosure Issues

Chapter Two Learning Objectives: When the student has completed this chapter he or she will be able to:

- Summarize the overriding thrust of Illinois Agency laws.
- Describe the principal duties licensees owe clients and customers.
- Highlight the essential disclosures licensees owe clients and customers when acting as a dual agent, designated agent and conventional single-agent
- Summarize the thrust of the brokerage agreement including "minimal services" and duties that survive closing
- Identify the principal requirements of the seller's property condition disclosure report and who is obligated to do what.
- Define and discuss the essential import of residential warranties and pre-closing inspections

Course Time: 3 Hrs.

===

Chapter 3: Fair Housing, Anti-Trust, and Other Anti-discrimination Laws

Chapter Three Learning Objectives: When the student has completed this chapter he or she will be able to:

- Summarize the purpose and thrust of the Illinois Human Rights Act
- Define and describe the principal forms of illegal discrimination
- Identify what parties are exempt from the fair housing prohibitions
- Describe how fair housing violations are enforced
- Summarize the key provisions of the Americans with Disabilities Act
- Define and summarize the principal forms of anti-trust legislation, including The Sherman Antitrust Act, Clayton Antitrust Act, collusion; price fixing; market allocation; and tie-in agreements

Course Time: 2.25 Hrs.

===

Chapter 4: Sales Contracts and Trust Funds

Chapter Four Learning Objectives: When the student has completed this chapter he or she will be able to:

- Define numerous legal characteristics of contract and sales contracts in particular, including validity; who may complete; contingencies; default; contract creation; and blank contracts
- Enumerate the essential requirements for compliant handling of trust fund deposits
- Summarize the various requirements for managing trust fund accounts

- List ways brokers can handle trust fund disputes and disputed disbursements
- Define the trust fund prohibitions of commingling and conversion
- Define and describe primary and secondary provisions of the sales contract

Course Time: 2.75 Hrs.

==

Chapter 5: Estimating Market Value

Chapter Five Learning Objectives: When the student has completed this chapter he or she will be able to:

- Define 'market value' and the pre-conditions for a valid market value estimate
- List the steps involved in the overall appraisal process encompassing the three approaches to value.
- Summarize the specific steps involved in generating a value estimate using the market data approach
- Identify how to complete a broker's comparative market analysis
- Describe the steps involved in the income approach to value

Course Time: 1.5 Hrs.

==

Chapter 6: Other Laws & Regulations Affecting Brokerage Functions

Chapter Six Learning Objectives: When the student has completed this chapter he or she will be able to:

- Define broker cooperation and describe generally how cooperation works in the context of the multiple listing services.
- Define 'teams' and highlight several areas of concern with teams that have become regulated..
- Identify forms of compensation and summarize the principal regulations surrounding compensation and how and when it can be legitimately received
- Summarize the principal regulations framing compliant real estate advertising practice, including identifications; web advertising; electronic communications and prohibitions
- Identify what activities unlicensed assistants can legally undertake
- Summarize what brokerage activities constitute 'licensed activities' requiring an active real estate license

Course Time: 1.5 Hrs.

==

INDEX OF INTERACTIVE EXERCISES

		IDPFR 15-hr stipulated interactive topics	
Role play/ situational case study examples			
Chapter 1	1	**Listing presentation, agreement, disclosures**	
Chapter 1	2	**Buyer representation, Agency, Disclosure**	
Chapter 1	3	**Presenting, negotiating, countering offers**	
Chapter 1	4	**Handling multiple offers and counteroffers**	
Chapter 2	5	**Designated agency disclosure / dual agency**	
Chapter 4	6	**Request writing purchase agreement / offer**	
Chapter 6	7	**Managing assistants**	
Demonstration Examples			
Chapter 1	1	**Seller net sheet**	
Chapter 1	2	**Buyer closing costs**	
Chapter 5	3	**Market Analysis**	
"What If" Situation Examples			
Chapter 2	1	**Distressed property issues**	
Chapter 2	2	**Inspection / repairs issues**	
Chapter 3	3	**Confronting fair housing violations /**	
		seller or buyer handling of failing contracts	
Chapter 3	4	**Fair housing questions**	
Chapter 3	5	**Anti-trust scenarios**	
Chapter 4	6	**Proper handling / disbursing escrow money**	

CHAPTER 1:
THE LISTING AND SELLING PROCESS

Chapter One Learning Objectives: When the student has completed this chapter he or she will be able to:

- Highlight the components of residential prospecting strategy.
- Summarize the key steps in planning and executing a listing presentation
- Identify the purpose and prevailing types of listing agreements
- Summarize the four benchmarks in the listing process
- Describe the key activities that take place prior to closing and the broker's responsibilities during this period
- Discuss the impact of electronic communications on residential brokerage, including MLS, emails, social media and smartphones
- Summarize essential advertising regulations framing one's brokerage practice
- Identify the principal elements and financial entries in the seller's net sheet.
- Calculate a buyer's estimated closing costs

Listings are the traditional source of a broker's income. By obtaining a listing, a broker obtains a share of the commission generated whenever a cooperating broker finds a buyer. By contrast, in working with a buyer, It is not so certain that the effort will produce income. In the absence of an exclusive buyer representation agreement, a buyer may move from one agent to another without making any commitment. Agents can spend considerable time with a buyer and earn nothing. Hence the special value of an exclusive listing with a seller: it is likely to generate revenue.

PROSPECTING

Prospecting is any activity designed to generate listing prospects: parties who intend to sell or lease property and who have not yet committed to a broker. Prospecting activities include mailing newsletters and flyers, selling person-to-person, advertising, and selling indirectly via community involvement. The goal of prospecting is to reach a potential seller or landlord, make that person aware of the agent's and brokerage's services, and obtain permission to discuss the benefits of listing, often in the form of a formal selling presentation.

Prospecting strategies

There are numerous ways to find listings and the most profitable options depend on the market and personality of the listing agent. If an agent is familiar with a particular neighborhood or they have a large network of colleagues, then focusing on marketing to these spheres of influence would be the most profitable way to find clients. This can be done with face-to-face meetings, phone calls, or handwritten cards.

When buyers and sellers are looking for a Realtor, they typically ask their friends first. This is why a referral-based lead generation objective is the most fruitful and sustainable. The leads are already "warm" and comfortable with being approached. Most agents strive to reach this stage of maturity in their business where they do not have to actively market to "cold" leads and can focus on their friends, family and past clientele.

Expireds and FSBOs. If the agent has yet to establish a network or a presence in their local market, then their efforts are better focused on direct outreach to build a database filled with future clients. Some of the more popular methods include cold calling expired listings and For Sale By Owners, or FSBOs.

Expired listings are homes that have had trouble selling with their original real estate agent. These listings are a great target because they are actively looking to sell. When calling expired listings it is important to come from a helpful angle and suggest what could be done differently in order to sell the home. There are paid services out there that offer the phone numbers and addresses of expired listings daily, and some brokerages offer these services to their agents.

Reaching out to FSBOs also requires some preparation and familiarity with common scripts. For Sale By Owners are typically people who are trying to save as much money as possible and believe they can handle everything themselves. These prospects can be found by driving around or by searching online or on social media.

Farming. Besides cold-calling expired listings and FSBOs, agents can also build their network by "farming" a specific neighborhood with mailers and door-knocking, hosting open houses for other agents, purchasing leads through online platforms like Zillow and Realtor.com and utilizing social media such as Facebook and Instagram.

When choosing a neighborhood to "farm", it is important to research the hottest areas. Where are most of the homes selling? Which neighborhoods have the largest turnover rates? The turnover rate can be calculated by adding up all of the sold homes in the last 12 months, and dividing it by the total number of homes. Depending on the market, this rate should be around 7 to 8%. But, before committing to a neighborhood, it is vital to check if there are other agents heavily farming that area or consistently listing homes. If there are a few agents with whom each listing is sold with, then that neighborhood will take longer and more effort to convert. Consider farming neighborhoods that do not have a preference for a given Realtor. One of the ways to find this out is by door-knocking a neighborhood and speaking with some of the current residents.

Once a neighborhood is picked, the agent has to develop a consistent marketing plan in order to see any results. By incorporating regular mailers (postcards, community event calendars, recipes, handwritten letters, market trends), door-knocking, door hangers, and special promotions, the agent will become accepted and trusted by the whole neighborhood. Farming takes consistent effort and time before showing results.

Open houses. An agent does not have to rely on their own listings in order to host an open house. The key to running a successful open house is picking one in a popular neighborhood where the leads are easy to convert. The busiest open houses are ones that have been aggressively pre-marketed for at least one week prior. Pre-marketing an open house can be done through posting on social media, delivering flyers to the neighbors, and door-knocking the surrounding homes with invites to the open house. Open houses are typically held on weekends between the hours of 11-4pm in order to allow for maximum traffic.

When hosting an open house, the goal is to capture the emails and phone numbers of the attendees with a sign-in sheet in order to follow-up with them in the future. The attendees rarely purchase the actual listing, but they are active buyers that literally come knocking on your door.

Open house leads usually take about 3-6 months to convert so it is important to stay on top of following up through phone calls, text messages, and emails.

In the current period, it is very common for agents to also utilize online platforms to build their pipelines. This can be done through social media or by purchasing leads through platforms like Zillow and Realtor.com. These platforms allow buyers to request showings directly through their websites and phone applications. The platform then captures the buyer's information and sends it to local agents who are purchasing leads for that particular zip code. These particular leads have to be responded to almost immediately and converted with a quick phone call or a text message.

THE LISTING PRESENTATION

The listing presentation is a chance for the listing agent to tour the home and showcase why the seller should list with them. Chances are, the seller will be interviewing multiple agents so it is important to be professional.

Preparations

The agent should come prepared with an estimated net sheet, a detailed marketing plan, and all of the necessary listing paperwork. During the property tour, the agent should ask specific questions about any upgrades the seller may have done, and the age of the major systems (AC, roof, plumbing, and electrical). Some listing appointments can be casual, for example during a happy hour, whereas others require a top-notch, formal presentation. The key is to adjust to the style of the owner. By mirroring the clients preferences, the agent can quickly adapt and make a better impression.

Optimize the property. During the listing presentation, the agent should discuss how to outshine other active listings. Present the property at its full potential. If possible, the sellers should add a fresh coat of paint and spruce up the landscaping for maximum curb appeal. During the listing presentation it is also vital to highlight the importance of a de-cluttered and clean home. Staging the property and providing professional photography will greatly impact the amount of traffic the listing will have. There are staging companies out there who focus on real estate listings, and there are also staging kits that can be purchased online with minor items to spruce up the showing potential of the home.

LISTING AGREEMENTS

The most common way of creating an agency relationship is by listing agreement. The agreement sets forth the various authorizations and duties, as well as requirements for compensation. A listing agreement establishes an agency for a specified transaction with a stated expiration.

A listing agreement, the document that puts an agent or broker in business, is a legally enforceable real estate agency agreement between a real estate broker and a client, authorizing the broker to perform a stated service for compensation. The unique characteristic of a listing agreement is that it is governed both by agency law and by contract law.

Scope of authority

Customarily, a listing is a special agency, or limited agency, agreement. Special agency limits the scope of the broker's authority to specific activities, generally those which generate customers and catalyze the transaction. A special agency agreement usually does not authorize a broker to obligate the client to a contract as a principal party, unless the agreement expressly grants such authorization, or the client has granted power of attorney to the broker. For example, a listing broker may not tell a buyer that the seller will accept an offer regardless of its terms. Telling the offeror that the offer is accepted would be an even more serious breach of the agreement.

Under agency law, a client is liable for actions the broker performs that are within the scope of authority granted by the listing agreement. A client is not liable for acts of the broker which go beyond the stated or implied scope of authority.

A broker may represent any principal party of a transaction: seller, landlord, buyer, tenant. An owner listing authorizes a broker to represent an owner or landlord.

Types of listing agreement

There are three main types of owner listing agreement:

1. exclusive right-to-sell (or lease)
2. exclusive agency
3. open listing.

Another type of listing, although legal yet frowned upon in Illinois, is a net listing. The first three forms differ in their statement of conditions under which the broker will be paid. The net listing is a variation on how much the broker will be paid.

Exclusive right-to-sell agreement. A buyer agency or tenant representation agreement authorizes a broker to represent a buyer or tenant. The most commonly used form is an exclusive right-to-represent agreement, the equivalent of an exclusive right-to-sell. However, exclusive agency and open types of agreement may be also used to secure a relationship on this side of a transaction.

The exclusive right-to-sell, also called an exclusive, is the most widely used owner agreement. Under the terms of this listing, a seller contracts exclusively with a single broker to procure a buyer or effect a sale transaction. If a buyer is procured during the listing period, the broker is entitled to a commission, regardless of who is procuring cause. Thus, if anyone--the owner, another broker-- sells the property, the owner must pay the listing broker the contracted commission.

The exclusive right-to-lease is a similar contract for a leasing transaction. Under the terms of this listing, the owner or landlord must pay the listing broker a commission if anyone procures a tenant for the named premises.

The exclusive listing gives the listing broker the greatest assurance of receiving compensation for marketing efforts.

In Illinois all exclusive listings must be in writing to be enforceable.

Exclusive agency. An exclusive agency listing authorizes a single broker to sell the property and earn a commission, but leaves the owner the right to sell the property without the broker's assistance, in which case no commission is owed. Thus, if any party other than the owner is procuring cause in a completed sale of the property, including another broker, the contracted broker has earned the commission.

Open listing. An open listing, or, simply, open, is a non-exclusive authorization to sell or lease a property. The owner may offer such agreements to any number of brokers in the marketplace. With an open listing, the broker who is the first to perform under the terms of the listing is the sole party entitled to a commission. Performance usually consists of being the procuring cause in the finding of a ready, willing, and able customer. If the transaction occurs without a procuring broker, no commissions are payable.

Open listings are rare in residential brokerage but relatively common in commercial brokerage. Residential brokers generally shy away from them because they offer no assurance of compensation for marketing efforts. In addition, open listings are more likely to cause commission disputes. To avoid such disputes, a broker has to register prospects with the owner to provide evidence of procuring cause in case a transaction results.

An open listing may be oral or written.

Net listing. A net listing is one in which an owner sets a minimum acceptable amount to be received from the transaction and allows the broker to have any amount received in excess as a commission, assuming the broker has earned a commission according to the other terms of the agreement. The owner's "net" may or may not account for closing costs.

For example, a seller requires $75,000 for a property. A broker sells the property for $83,000 and receives the difference, $8,000, as commission.

Net listings are generally regarded as unprofessional today, although legal in Illinois many states have outlawed them. The argument against the net listing is that it creates a conflict of interest for the broker. It is in the broker's interest to encourage the owner to put the lowest possible acceptable price in the listing, regardless of market value. Thus the agent violates fiduciary duty by failing to place the client's interests above those of the agent.

LISTING BENCHMARKS

Determining a price

It is almost always necessary for an agent seeking a listing to suggest a listing price or price range for the property. It is important to make a careful estimate, because underpricing a property is not in the best interests of the seller, and overpricing it often prevents a transaction altogether. In brief, an agent usually relies on an analysis of comparable properties which have recently sold in the same neighborhood. By making adjustments for the differences between the subject property and the comparables, the agent arrives at a general price range. Agents must be careful to caution sellers that they are not appraisers, and that the suggested price range is not an expert opinion of market value. If a more precise estimate of market value is desired, the seller should hire a licensed appraiser.

Marketing listings

The process of marketing a listed property leads to the desired end of a completed sale contract. During this process, there are critical skills an agent must master during the key phases of marketing plan implementation, selling the buyer prospect, and obtaining an accepted offer..

After the broker formalizes the listing agreement, the agent initiates a marketing plan for the property. An ideal marketing plan is a cohesive combination of promotional and selling activities directed at potential customers. The best combination is one that aims to have maximum impact on the marketplace in relation to the time and money expended.

Professional photography of a home will help garner more attention. Besides photography, professional videos can be filmed, and a Matterport camera can be used in order to share the floorplan with potential buyers.

Once the listing is on the market, the true work begins. Besides "shouting from the rooftops" that a listing is live, there are actual strategies to share a listing with the local market. Broker's opens are open houses geared towards agents only so they can preview the home to see if it is a good fit for their buyers. These are common with luxury listings. Besides broker's opens, cold calling local agents, delivering door hangers to the neighbors, hosting open houses and running social media advertisements will help get more eyes on the listing as well. Real estate is a numbers game, and the sooner a listing is seen by a majority of agents, the faster it will sell.

Selling the buyer prospect

When marketing activities produce prospects, the agent's marketing role becomes more interpersonal. An agent must now:

- qualify prospects' plans, preferences, and financial capabilities
- show properties that meet the customer's needs
- elicit the buyer's reactions to properties
- report material results to the seller or listing agent

At the earliest appropriate time, an agent must make certain disclosures to a prospective customer. An agent is required to disclose the relevant agency relationship, the property's physical condition, and the possible presence of hazardous materials.

Obtaining offers

If a buyer is interested in purchasing a property, an agent obtains the buyer's offer of transaction terms, including price, down payment, desired closing date, and financing requirements. An agent must be extremely careful at this point to abide by statutory obligations to the client, whoever that party may be. Discussions of price are particularly delicate: whether the client is buyer or seller, the agent's duty is to uphold the client's best interests. Thus, it is not acceptable to suggest to a customer what price the client will or will not accept. With pricing and other issues, it is always a good practice to understand what role the client wants the agent to assume in the offering phase of the transaction; in other words, exactly how far the agent may go in developing terms on the client's behalf.

When a buyer or tenant makes an offer, the agent must present it to the seller or landlord at the earliest possible moment. If the terms of the offer are unacceptable, the agent may assist the seller in developing a counteroffer, which the agent would subsequently submit to the customer or customer's agent. The offering and counteroffering process continues until a meeting of the minds results in a sale contract.

Multiple offers. Multiple offer situations are common in seller's markets. If a listing is priced well, in good condition and in a hot area, then it will sell quickly and may result in a bidding war. Multiple offers can be difficult to organize, but one strategy is to call for a "highest and best" offer from all of the agents. This will save time from going back and forth with each agent and ensure that the offers are the strongest option a buyer is willing to make.

Presenting offers. Once all of the new offers are in, organizing the important terms in an Excel sheet is a helpful way to present the offers to the sellers.

The important terms to organize are as follows:

- purchase price
- earnest money deposit
- financing type (cash, conventional, FHA, VA, USDA)
- downpayment amount
- length of inspection period
- closing date
- incentives (are the buyer's asking for any closing cost assistance?)
- miscellaneous additional terms

PRE-CLOSING ACTIVITIES

Hopefully, the marketing plan, prospect selling and offer presentations generates an executed contract. At this point, between the execution of the sale contract and the closing of the transaction, the property is "under contract" or "contract pending." During this period, buyer and seller have certain things to do to achieve a successful closing. The buyer often needs to arrange financing and dispose of other property; the seller may need to clear up title encumbrances and make certain property repairs. The sale contract should specify all such required tasks. The time period between contracting and closing is referred to as the contingency period, or pre-closing period.

Broker responsibilities

As dictated by custom and the circumstances of a transaction, an agent has a range of duties and responsibilities during the pre-closing period. An agent's foremost duty following acceptance of an offer is to submit the contract and the earnest money to the sponsoring broker without delay. In Illinois, earnest money must be deposited within twenty-four hours after the time of acceptance of a sales contract.

The agent must also complete their due diligence in the listing. This refers to verifying the accuracy of the statements in the listing regarding the property, the owner, and the owner's representations. Especially important facts for a broker to verify are:

- the property condition
- ownership status
- the client's authority to act

Failure to perform a reasonable degree of due diligence may increase an agent's exposure to liability in the event that the property is not as represented or that the client cannot perform as promised.

Other responsibilities are:

- assisting the buyer in obtaining financing
- recommending inspectors, appraisers, attorneys, and title companies
- assisting in communications between principals
  assisting in the exchange of transaction documents

Waiting for the inspection and appraisal results is one of the most stressful times in a real estate transaction. There are so many moving parts and these two reports can completely alter the trajectory of the transaction. An inspection period is the time the buyers have to complete their due diligence and review any inspections that have been ordered for the home. Oftentimes, buyers will request repairs to be completed that are not necessary for insurance purposes so a listing agent's job is to negotiate with the buyers and keep their sellers from completing any unnecessary repairs. A buyer's agents job is to fight for the buyers and negotiate for any repairs they deem necessary.

Not all inspection results are positive, and sometimes a deal has to fall through due to the buyers wanting to move on from the property. In this case, a contract cancellation addendum should be sent to all parties to sign.

The appraisal could also lead to some stress. A third party completes the appraisal by picking comparable properties, and ensuring the safety and condition of the home. Different financing types have different appraisal criteria so it is important to let both the inspector and appraiser know what financing is being used.

If an appraisal comes in below the purchase price with required repairs (i.e. a piece of wood rot was found), then all parties have to come together and work through the issues. Either the buyer will have to come to the closing table with cash to cover the difference or the seller will have to lower the price. Another option is that the seller and buyer split the difference amongst themselves. In regards to any property damage that needs to be fixed for an appraisal, that will have to be negotiated between both parties as well. Once everything is agreed upon and fixed, then a re-appraisal occurs to confirm that the necessary repairs have been made.

The culmination of the pre-closing period -- and all its diligence activities -- is a successful closing where the parties exchange consideration and title, and the transaction is consummated. At this point the sale contract is successfully extinguished.

COMMUNICATIONS AND TECHNOLOGY

Multiple listing services (MLS) and websites

The posting and sharing of property listings and data among broker websites, firm websites, and multiple listing services (MLS) is one of the most effective marketing tools available to today's licensees. Broker cooperation assures sellers of maximum exposure for their properties, just as it assures buyers of seeing the widest possible range of listed properties. This system is used for leases, income properties, and residential homes. The MLS contains pertinent information for agents including public record details on the property, commission offered, and open house dates.

To ensure fair use of MLS facilities, the National Association of REALTORS® has developed an Internet Data Exchange (IDX) policy that enables MLS members to display and use MLS data while respecting the rights of property owners and brokers to market their properties however they want. Basically, persons who want to make use of MLS data have to share their own data as well. They can opt out of the sharing policy so that competitors cannot post their properties on competing websites, but then they cannot post competitors' properties on their own sites.

There are a number of websites that provide consumers with the capability to search through listings all over the country and even the world. Of course, it is always wise to recognize that information posted on the internet is not necessarily reliable and that the source of the information should be considered carefully.

In other words, the MLS syndicates with hundreds of websites so the public can get access to current market listings as well. Some of the more popular websites it sends listings to are Zillow, Realtor.com, Redfin, and Trulia. The listings sometimes lag when they are published but usually show up within a day or two.

Most buyers in today's market prefer using the aforementioned websites, but the MLS also has a phone application that agents can share with their clients. Some brokerages have also been investing more of their money into technology and developed their own phone applications that are worth sharing with clients.

Email and texting

Frequent and virtually instantaneous contact between real estate practitioners and consumers is possible via email and texting. As both these forms of communication fall under the category of advertising, practitioners need to carefully observe their state's advertising regulations. In brief, be truthful, direct, and concise. Provide the information required by law, and do not violate prohibitions against unsolicited emails and messages.

Social media

Social media websites allow rapid exchange of information, documents, photos, messages and data with a select group of contacts. They also represent another form of advertising and so are subject to real estate commission advertising regulations in most states.

Another digital form of marketing that is growing popularity is social media. There are many platforms to choose from- LinkedIn, Facebook, Instagram, and TikTok are the most common ones. These platforms allow agents to stay in touch with their database in a subtle way and educate their audience on the real estate market. Constantly engaging with people through these platforms will add another source of lead generation and help grow the transaction pipeline. If possible, having a presence on all platforms is advisable, but most likely the agent will find one they resonate with the most and focus their attention there.

Smartphones

Smartphones facilitate the use, not only of email, texting, and social media, but also of immediate internet access, document review, photo and document sharing, data storage, and video conferencing. They offer, in fact, an almost complete mobile office.

Managing information

The ability to satisfy the needs of clients and customers is largely dependent on a broker's ability to obtain, organize, and manage information. Information is a cornerstone of the broker's perceived value in the marketplace and a major reason why buyers and sellers seek a broker out. Systematic collection and updating of relevant information is therefore a business priority.

Property data

Most brokerages maintain two categories of property data: available properties, and all properties in the market area. In residential brokerage, available property basically consists of the listings in the MLS and for-sale-by-owner properties. Records for all properties in an area are accessible in tax records. Commercial brokerages usually keep track of available and occupied commercial properties in a proprietary database.

Buyer data

Buyer information is usually compiled and maintained, often informally, by each agent in a brokerage. An agency's base of prospects who are looking for property at any given time is valuable for marketing new listings.

Tenant data

In residential and commercial leasing companies, information is compiled and maintained on all tenants in an area, by property type used. Such files contain a tenant's lease expiration, property size, and rent.

Client data

It is important to keep track of both current and former clients. Former clients are likely prospects to become clients again or customers. They are also a source of referrals. Current clients, of course, should be the broker's primary concern.

Market data

Today's clients and customers expect a broker to know the market intimately. It is often the broker with the best market knowledge who dominates business in the market. Knowing a market includes keeping up to date on:

- pricing and appreciation trends

- financing rates and terms
- demographic patterns and trends
- construction trends
- general economic trends

ADVERTISEMENT REGULATIONS

Advertising is an important tool in marketing properties and procuring buyers. It is, however, subject to regulation and restrictions. In general, state laws and regulations require that:

- advertising must not be misleading
- the sponsoring and managing broker is responsible for the content of advertising done by agents
- all advertising must reveal the identity of the brokerage firm; licensee may not use blind ads that conceal their identities
- brokers selling their own property through the brokerage must disclose the brokerage identity
- licensees must include the broker's business identity in any advertising; they may not advertise in their own name solely (unless selling their own property through channels other than the agency)

Telephone Consumer Protection Act

The TCPA (Telephone Consumer Protection Act) addresses the regulation of unsolicited telemarketing phone calls. Rules include the following:

- telephone solicitors must identify themselves, on whose behalf they are calling, and how they can be contacted
- telemarketers must comply with any do-not-call request made during the solicitation call
- consumers can place their home and wireless phone numbers on a national Do-Not-Call list which prohibits future solicitations from telemarketers.

CAN-SPAM Act

The CAN-SPAM Act (Controlling the Assault of Non-Solicited Pornography and Marketing Act of 2003) supplements the Telephone Consumer Protection Act (TCPA). It

- bans sending unwanted email 'commercial messages' to wireless devices
- requires express prior authorization
- requires giving an 'opt out' choice to terminate the sender's messages

When attending a listing consultation, most sellers will ask for a net sheet with an estimate of their net proceeds after all of the mortgage payoffs, closing costs and commissions. Most title companies and law offices will provide branded ones for agents, or it can be done manually.

===

Check Your Understanding Challenges:

Chapter One: The Listing and Selling Process

Carefully read each question then provide your best answer based on what you learned in this chapter. Then check your answers against the Answer Key which immediately follows the chapter questions.

1. A new licensee is developing a strategy to generate business in a defined market area in her community. Which of the following strategies would you adopt for optimum results toward your goal of capturing buyers and sellers?

   A.   An email campaign to new residents promoting newer properties.
   B.   A word-of-mouth strategy to neighborhood community groups to generate referrals.
   C.   A direct selling approach in an established neighborhood to generate long-time residents and buyers desiring established neighborhoods.
   D.   Develop a farm geography where there is a strong business presence, since employment centers employ the most qualified buyers.

2. List three critical criteria for defining and setting up a prospecting farm.

   1.   _____

   2.   _____

   3.   _____

3. List four specific preparations to complete prior to engaging in a listing presentation.

   1. _____

   2. _____

   3. _____

   4. _____

4. What are the two principal considerations to be aware of in pricing a listing, and how can licensees ultimately defend the listing price they propose?:

   Consideration (1):   _____

   _____

   Consideration (2):   _____

How defend price estimate? _____

_____

_____

5. How would you define what constitutes the optimum marketing plan on a given listing in terms of activities and objectives?

The optimum marketing plan is one which _____

_____

_____

6. In general, overall terms, what are the principal calculations involved in preparing a seller's net sheet?

_____

_____

_____

7. Which of the following brokerage agreement offers the brokerage firm the fullest protection regarding the payment of compensation in the event that the seller sells to a neighbor?

   a.   Open listing
   b.   Exclusive right to sell
   c.   Net listing
   d.   Multiple listing

8. If you are the listing broker working on an offer with a customer, what are the two critical guidelines to follow in dealing with the sensitive pricing issue?

        Guideline A: _____

        Guideline B: _____

9. During the pre-closing process, an important facet of the due diligence the broker must perform is verifying the seller's statements and representations. What are three other broker responsibilities that must be discharged during this phase?

    1. _____

    2. _____

    3. _____

10. There are five overriding thrusts of advertising regulation that comprise the foundations of acceptable residential brokerage practice in Illinois. Name three of these foundations.

    1. _____

    2. _____

    3. _____

Answer Key: Check Your Understanding Challenges

Chapter One: The Listing and Selling Process

1. A new licensee is developing a strategy to generate business in a defined market area in her community. Which of the following strategies would you adopt for optimum results toward your goal of capturing buyers and sellers?

   b. **A word-of-mouth strategy to neighborhood community groups to generate referrals.**

   Tailor your prospecting and listing efforts to maximize your opportunities to generate referrals. Most agents strive to develop a referral base as this capitalizes on the trust you've generated through past efforts.

2. List three critical criteria for defining and setting up a prospecting farm.

   1. Select a high-growth market area

   2. Select a market area with a high turnover rate

   3. Select a market area that is not over-saturated with competitors and does not have a preference for a given licensee.

3. List four specific preparations to complete prior to engaging in a listing presentation.

   1. A seller's net sheet

   2. A detailed marketing plan

   3. Sample agreements and other documents

   4. A questionnaire for the seller to ascertain data on property condition

4. What are the two principal considerations to be aware of in pricing a listing, and how can licensees ultimately defend the listing price they propose?:

   Consideration (1):   do not underprice as you will short your client

   Consideration (2):   do not overprice as the listing won't sell at all

   How defend price estimate? Perform a comprehensive CMA that can generate seller reliance based on the general validity of the principle of substitution in valuing residential properties. That principle holds that buyers will buy a property if it is priced comparably to other nearby similar homes.

5. How would you define what constitutes the optimum marketing plan on a given listing in terms of activities and objectives?

   The optimum marketing plan is one which combines any number of promotional activities and selling activities targeted at potential customers that aims to have maximum impact on the marketplace in relation to the time and money expended.

6. In general, overall terms, what are the principal calculations involved in preparing a seller's net sheet?

From the purchase price, subtract the broker's commission, the loan balance, and seller-owed expenses, then add back any prorated credits owed the seller.

7. Which of the following brokerage agreement offers the brokerage firm the fullest protection regarding the payment of compensation in the event that the seller sells to a neighbor?

B. Exclusive right to sell

8. If you are the listing broker working on an offer with a customer, what are the two critical professional practice guidelines to follow in moving the transaction to the next phase?

Guideline A: Do not suggest what price the seller will or will not accept; stick to the listing price!

Guideline B: Present the offer to the seller at the earliest opportunity and assist with a counteroffer if necessary

9. During the pre-closing process, an important facet of the due diligence the broker must perform is verifying the seller's statements and representations. What are three other broker responsibilities that must be discharged during this phase?

1. **assisting the buyer in procuring financing**

2. **recommending inspectors, appraisers, title companies**

3. **facilitating communications and document flow between principals**

10. There are five overriding thrusts of advertising regulation that comprise the foundations of acceptable residential brokerage practice in Illinois. Name three of these foundations.

1. **advertising must not be misleading**

2. **the sponsoring and managing broker are responsible for all ad content**

3. **all advertising must reveal the identity of the brokerage firm; licensee may not use blind ads that conceal their identities**

4. **brokers selling their own property through the brokerage must disclose the brokerage identity**

5. **licensees must include the broker's business identity in any advertising as they may not advertise solely in their own name**

INTERACTIVE EXERCISES

CHAPTER 1: THE LISTING AND SELLING PROCESS

ROLE PLAY / SITATIONAL CASE STUDY 1: Listing presentation, agreement, disclosures

After weeks of cold-calling expired listings, Sally finally lands a listing appointment for the following Tuesday. Over the next few days, she works on preparing a lengthy listing presentation, compiling a Comparative Market Analysis (CMA) to determine a price, and developing a personalized marketing plan until she feels ready to tackle her first listing appointment. Tuesday finally arrives and after a night of tossing and turning Sally puts on a brave face and drives across town to the appointment.

The seller greets Sally at the door but immediately apologizes that his wife could not be there because she had a prior commitment. He then shows Sally around the home, highlighting the upgrades he has done over the last few years and asking questions about Sally's expertise.

Sally had prepared for those questions and references her company's success in the local market and fields every hardball inquiry with dignity and grace. She confidently goes over the CMA, the listing price and her marketing plan and just as she's about to move on to the listing agreement, he stops her.

She knew things were going too well and he shocks her by letting her know he is meeting with a few other agents and would like to pursue a net listing with all of them. So essentially, a net *and* open listing. The agent who brings him the highest priced offer will get the highest commission. He has been scarred in the past by agents who just put a yard sign into the yard, upload the listing on the MLS and then call it quits.

What did Sally do wrong? How can she fix this situation? How could Sally have prevented this?

_____

_____

_____

_____

_____

_____

_____

_____

_____

_____

Case Debrief:

The first mistake Sally made was she did not ensure that both homeowners would be present at the listing presentation. This is vital because it is easier to field any questions they both have and tackle things head on. Also, with both owners present they are able to sign the paperwork right then and there, otherwise Sally will have to leave it with them and wait until the other seller reads through everything.

Sally's second mistake was avoiding the discussion of different types of listing agreements. In the future, she can prevent this by explaining to the sellers the most common types of listing agreements and how they benefit the sellers.

Now that she is in this situation, she should thoroughly discuss why an open and net listing would be detrimental to the sellers. Open listings are rare in residential brokerage. Brokers generally shy away from them because they offer no assurance of compensation for marketing efforts. In addition, open listings cause commission disputes. To avoid such disputes, a broker has to register prospects with the owner to provide evidence of procuring cause in case a transaction results. This will create more hassle and involvement from the seller. It also can lead to brokers focusing less on the listing since they do not have a guaranteed payday at the end.

Net listings are generally regarded as unprofessional today, although legal in Illinois many states have outlawed them. The argument against the net listing is that it creates a conflict of interest for the broker. It is in the broker's interest to encourage the owner to put the lowest possible acceptable price in the listing, regardless of market value. Thus the agent violates fiduciary duty by failing to place the client's interests above those of the agent.

==

ROLE PLAY / SITATIONAL CASE STUDY 2: Buyer representation, agency, disclosure

Andrew has been searching high and low for the right home for his client. Unfortunately, his client is extremely picky and is looking for a needle in a haystack. When Andrew hears that his colleague Francesca is listing a home that meets 95% of Andrew's requirements, he immediately sends it to his client and asks if he'd like to see it before it goes live on the market.

His client sees it, falls in love with it but wants to ask for a 2% closing cost contribution from the sellers. Since Andrew is friends with Francesca he openly tells her that his client doesn't actually *need* that 2% and that he would settle for a smaller contribution. Andrew is tired of lugging his client around and wants him to go under contract ASAP. So, Francesca and her clients submit a counter-offer with zero seller contributions. Andrew explains to his client that the sellers have a bottom-line and that this counter-offer is their best bet, so his client accepts it and they go under contract.

Upon closing, Andrew's client is shocked to find out that the sellers are actually profiting $65,000. He reaches out to Francesca and asks her why they lied about their bottom line. She spills the beans and Andrew's client is furious that his agent went behind his back.

Was Andrew in the wrong? Can his client file a complaint with his broker?

_____

_____

_____

_____

_____

_____

_____

_____

_____

Case Debrief:

As a buyer's agent, Andrew had to remain loyal to his client and keep his situation confidential. By revealing to Francesca that his client could indeed afford those closing costs, he broke both of those fiduciary duties. Loyalty means he has to place the interests of the client above those of all others, particularly the agent's own. In this particular situation he definitely did not uphold his client's best interest. He did not fight for the contribution for his client and ended up costing him more money.

By revealing the truth about his financial situation, Andrew directly broke the duty of confidentiality. An agent must hold in confidence any personal or business information received from the client during the term of employment. An agent may not disclose any information that would harm the client's interests or bargaining position, or anything else the client wishes to keep secret.

In the future, Andrew should be upfront with his client about what a strong offer is and fight tooth and nail to get their offer accepted. He should not have showed his playing cards to Francesca and ruined their bargaining position.

==

ROLE PLAY / SITATIONAL CASE STUDY 3: Presenting, negotiating, countering offers

Peoria is a hot seller's market and Emily's new listing has 12 offers. After organizing each offer by the important terms (price, financing type, closing date, etc), Emily narrows down the top 3 offers. She is obligated to present all offers to her clients, but she is ready to advise them on the ones she deems to be the strongest offers.

After presenting all of the offers, Emily is pleased to find out that her sellers agree with her on the top 3. They have a few terms they want to negotiate so she then sets forth to call those 3 agents. The agent with the best offer shares a heart-wrenching story of her client's home-search. That agent couldn't be there for the showing so Emily caves and reveals to that agent that the home actually has had signs of mold but the sellers are not willing to disclose it on the property disclosure. She could not have it on her conscience for those buyers to move in when there has been mold present.

A few hours later, the second two best offers update their terms more favorably and the agent with the number one offer revokes their contract. Emily's sellers are confused why they would do that but don't think twice and go under contract with another buyer. After all, they ended up receiving a much higher price than they originally imagined.

What did Emily do wrong?

_____

_____

_____

_____

_____

_____

_____

_____

_____

You might think that Emily disobeyed her clients when in reality, she acted properly by disclosing the defects to that agent. But, she should have disclosed the property issues to each agent who offered and viewed the property.

Agents do have certain obligations to customers, even though they do not represent them. In general, they owe a third party: honesty and fair dealing; reasonable care and skill; and proper disclosure. An agent has a duty to deal fairly and honestly with a customer. Thus, an agent may not deceive, defraud, or otherwise take advantage of a customer. Emily did the right thing by sharing the defects with that agent but she owed it to all 12 of the agents.

Emily should have also stressed to the sellers the importance of disclosing every material defect of the home. When they refused to do so, she should have taken the situation to her broker. Taking on listings where sellers force you to be shady is not worth the money. Emily can get into a lot of trouble over this mishap.

==

ROLE PLAY / SITATIONAL CASE STUDY 4: Handling multiple offers and counteroffers

Think back to Emily's Peoria listing. Did you know that one of the best offers was actually being presented by her best friend? This hot listing sure landed Emily in a lot of trouble. When she realized her best friend was offering on this home, she should have put her blinders on and not fallen for her mind's tricks.

Emily presented her seller's counteroffer but in doing so, she let slip that the other best offer was currently $5,000 higher than her best friends'.

What did Emily do wrong here?

_____

_____

_____

_____

_____

_____

_____

_____

_____

Case Debrief:

By revealing the status of the other offers **only** to her friend, Emily did not act fairly with all of the other agents and their customers. Emily also risked the potential that her sellers could have benefited from a better offer. If Emily had not told her friend, perhaps her friend would have offered $7,000 higher. Now that her friend knew they just had to offer at least $5,000 more, they had a leg up on the other agents.

Since her friend could potentially have offered a higher price, Emily's sellers might have missed out on some money. Emily did not have her client's best interest at heart.

===

DEMONSTRATION EXAMPLE 1: Seller's Net Sheet

Read the case scenario then complete the following worksheet to determine what the net proceeds are for the seller.

Molly and Sam Alders have accepted an offer on their house located at 4284 Maple Street. The buyers, Joe and Corinn Walters, offered $350,000, with earnest money of $3,500, down payment of $70,000 and the remaining $276,500 of the purchase price to come from a new conventional loan from Elm Mortgage Company. The loan is for 30 years at 4.5% interest, with a monthly principal plus interest payment of $1,419. The lender is charging no points and a 1.5% origination fee. Closing is set to occur at Capital Title Company at 4 p.m. on May 10 of the current year. Seller owns the day of closing.

The Alders have an agreement to pay a broker's commission of 6% to Magnolia Realty. Their unpaid mortgage loan balance as of May 1 will be $204,000. Their monthly interest payments are $780.00. The annual interest rate is 4%. The previous year's county taxes, amounting to $2,572, have been paid by the seller in arrears. The current year's taxes, not yet billed or paid, are assumed to be the same as the previous year's. The parties agree to prorate using the 365-day method, and that the day of closing belongs to the seller. The relevant facts and costs, and who pays them according to the terms of the sale contract, are summarized below.

Seller's Net Proceeds Worksheet

Sale price: _____

Deposit/down payment: _____

Loan amount: _____

The commission paid by the seller is: _____

Real estate taxes (paid in arrears) (assume 365-day method; prorated for the seller): _____

Seller's unpaid mortgage interest (assume 31 days): _____

Seller-paid costs (not necessarily all expenses in real world!)

    Commissions: _____

    Real estate taxes: _____

    Title insurance: $900 owner's coverage

Seller's attorney: $1,500

Record Release Deed: $25

Survey: $550

Transfer stamps: state and county: $324

Seller's loan payoff: _____

Total Costs:_____

Seller's total net proceeds: _____

==

Case Debrief

CALCULATING THE SELLER'S NET PROCEEDS

Sale price: $350,000

Deposit/down payment: $70,000

Loan amount: $276,500

The commission paid by the seller is: $350,000 x 6% = $21,000.00

Real estate taxes (paid in arrears; prorated expense for the seller): $916.50

Real estate taxes:

Using the 365-day method, the daily amount is $2,572 ÷ 365, or $7.05 (rounded). The total number of days is the number of days in January, February, March and April, plus 10 days in May, or (31+28+31+30+10), or 130 days. At closing, the seller's share of $916.50 is charged to the seller and the buyer is credited with the same amount.

Total amount due: = $ 2,572.00

Daily amount: = 2,572 ÷ 365 = $7.05

Seller's share   = 7.051 x 130 = $916.50

Seller's unpaid mortgage interest: $251.60

Daily amount: $780 ÷ 31 days = $25.16

Seller's charge: $25.16 x 10 days = 251.60

Seller-paid costs (not necessarily all expenses in real world!)

  Commissions: $21,000

  Real estate taxes: $916.50

  Mortgage interest: $251.60

  Title insurance: $900 owner's coverage

  Seller's attorney: $1,500

  Record Release Deed: $25

  Survey: $550

  Transfer stamps: state and county: $324

  Total Seller-paid costs: 25,467.10

Seller's loan payoff: $204,251.60

  Loan payoff: $204,000

  Interest: (daily amount = 780 ÷ 31 days = $25.16) x 10 days = $251.60

Total Costs: $229,718.70

  (seller-paid costs + loan payoff)

Seller's total net proceeds: $120,281.30

  (Price – total costs), or ($350,000 – 229, 718.70)

So, the seller's total net proceeds are calculated by subtracting all of their combined expenses ($229,718.70) from their gross purchase price ($350,000) to result in $120,281.30.

===

DEMONSTRATION EXAMPLE 2: Buyer's Closing costs

Read the case scenario then complete the following worksheet to determine what the buyers closing costs are.

Molly and Sam Alders have accepted an offer on their house located at 4284 Maple Street. The buyers, Joe and Corinn Walters, offered $350,000, with earnest money of $3,500, down payment of $70,000 and the remaining $276,500 of the purchase price to come from a new conventional loan from Elm Mortgage Company. The loan is for 30 years at 4.5% interest, with a monthly principal plus interest payment of $1,419. The lender is charging no points and a 1.5% origination fee. Closing is set to occur at Capital Title Company at 4 p.m. on May 10 of the current year.

The Alders have an agreement to pay a broker's commission of 6% to Magnolia Realty. Their unpaid mortgage loan balance as of May 1 will be $204,000. Their monthly interest payments are $780.00. The annual interest rate is 4%. The previous year's county taxes, amounting to $2,572, have been paid by the seller in arrears. The current year's taxes, not yet billed or paid, are assumed to be the same as the previous year's. The parties agree to prorate using the 365-day method, and that the day of closing belongs to the seller. The downpayment will be paid into escrow prior to closing.

The relevant facts and costs, and who pays them according to the terms of the sale contract, are summarized below.

Fill out the following worksheet to determine what the buyer's closing costs:

Buyer's Closing Costs Worksheet

Buyer costs / cost assumptions:

Appraisal fee:	$500
Credit report:	$50
Closing fee:	$450
Recording fees:	$55
Title insurance:	$250 for lender's coverage
Buyer's attorney:	$1,600
Pest inspection:	$100
Buyer's loan costs:	
points:	_____
origination fee:	_____
Hazard insurance:	$1,800 payable at closing
Real estate taxes:	_____
	($2,572.00, to be prorated)
Tax, insurance escrow:	_____
	(8 months' taxes, 4 months' insurance)
Prepaid loan interest:	_____

(daily interest times 21 days)

Buyer's Total Closing Costs: _____

(closing costs – closing credits)

===

Case Debrief:

Buyer's Closing Costs Worksheet

Buyer- paid Costs:

Appraisal fee:	$500
Credit report:	$50
Closing fee:	$450
Recording fees:	$55
Title insurance:	$250 for lender's coverage
Buyer's attorney:	$1,600
Pest inspection:	$100

Buyer's loan costs:

points:	0
origination fee:	$4,147.50

Hazard insurance: $1,800 payable at closing

Real estate taxes: ($916.50) credit to buyer

($2,572 ÷ 365 days = $7.05/day x 130 days = 916.50 credit to buyer)

Tax + insurance escrow: $2,314.64

($214.33 taxes/mo. x 8 months = $1,714.64) + (150/mo insurance x 4 months = $600) or $2,314.64

Prepaid loan interest: $702.40

(276,500 x 4.5% ÷ 12 = $1,036.88 interest/month;

divided by 31 = $33.45 interest/day x 21 days)

34

Buyer's Total Closing Costs: **$11,053.04**

(closing costs – closing credits)

==

CHAPTER 2:

AGENCY AND DISCLOSURE ISSUES

Chapter Two Learning Objectives: When the student has completed this chapter he or she will be able to:

- Summarize the overriding thrust of Illinois Agency laws.
- Describe the principal duties licensees owe clients and customers.
- Highlight the essential disclosures licensees owe clients and customers when acting as a dual agent, designated agent and conventional single-agent
- Summarize the thrust of the brokerage agreement including "minimal services" and duties that survive closing
- Identify the principal requirements of the seller's property condition disclosure report and who is obligated to do what.
- Define and discuss the essential import of residential warranties and pre-closing inspections

ILLINOIS AGENCY LAW

The Illinois Law of Agency covers how licensees may represent clients and the duties to those clients. The party being represented is the client, or principal, of the licensee. The law also delineates duties owed to parties who are unrepresented by the licensee (customers).

Because common law has sometimes resulted in misunderstandings and actions adverse to the best interests of the public, Article 15 clearly states that Illinois agency duties are not common law duties, but are, instead, those duties stated in the Act (Sec. 15-5).

Duties owed to clients

General duties. A licensee who represents a client must

- perform the terms of the brokerage agreement between the broker and client
- promote the client's best interests
- exercise reasonable skill and care when performing brokerage services
- keep confidential all confidential information received from the client

Promote client's interests. Promoting the client's best interests specifically means

- seek a transaction at the price and terms stated in the brokerage agreement
- present all offers to and from the client in a timely manner
- disclose material facts to the client that the licensee has actual knowledge
- account for money and property received
- obey all lawful instructions of the client
- acting in a way that promotes the client's best interests

Confidentiality. The Rules specify that licensees who receive confidential information must take reasonable steps to safeguard that information. Confidential information includes that which

- is obtained from a client during the term of a brokerage agreement that was made confidential by the client's written request or instruction
- deals with the client's negotiating position
- might materially harm the client's negotiating position if disclosed

Permitted activities. The licensee can show alternative properties to buyers or tenants, or show properties a client is interested in to other prospective buyers or tenants without breaching licensee duties.

The licensee may also present contemporaneous offers on the same property without breaching duties to the client.

Duties owed to customers

Licensees must treat all customers honestly and not give them false information knowingly or negligently.

Disclosures.

- **Relationship**. A licensee must disclose in writing to a customer that the licensee is not acting as the customer's agent before the customer discloses confidential information, but never later than preparing an offer or lease.
- **Property condition**. A seller's agent must disclose to prospective buyer customers, in a timely manner, all material facts relative to the physical condition of the property known to the licensee and that could not be discovered by a reasonably diligent inspection by the customer.
- **Liability**. The licensee is not liable to a customer for providing false information if that information was provided by the client and the licensee had no knowledge the information was false (Sec. 15-25)

Dual agency

In a dual agency, a single licensee represents both parties to a transaction, or two brokers licensed under the same sponsoring broker severally represent the two parties. A licensee is prohibited from serving as a dual agent in any transaction where the licensee or an entity in which the licensee has or will have any ownership interest, is a party to the transaction

Disclosure and consent. A licensee may act as a dual agent only with the informed, written consent of all parties. Dual agency disclosure must be presented to the client at the time the brokerage agreement is entered into and may be signed by the client at that time or at any time before the licensee acts as a dual agent for the client.

Permitted activities as dual agent.

- Treat all clients honestly.
- Provide information about the property to the buyer or tenant.

- Disclose all latent material defects of the property that are known to the licensee.
- Disclose financial qualifications of the buyer or tenant to the seller or landlord.
- Explain real estate terms.
- Help the buyer or tenant arrange for property inspections.
- Explain closing costs and procedures.
- Help the buyer compare financing options.
- Provide information about comparable properties that have sold so both clients may make educated decisions on what price to accept or offer.

This dual agency disclosure must be presented to the client at the time the brokerage agreement is entered into and may be signed by the client at that time or at any time before the licensee acts as a dual agent for the client.

Designated agency

Creation. When a licensee is working with a consumer, the licensee is assumed to be representing the consumer as a designated agent unless the sponsoring broker and consumer enter into a written agreement specifying a different relationship (Sec. 15-10).

A sponsoring broker entering into an agreement to represent a consumer in buying, selling, renting, leasing or exchanging property must specifically designate sponsored licensee(s) to act as the legal agent(s) of that consumer to the exclusion of all other licensees affiliated or employed by the sponsoring broker. The designated agent is the only company licensee representing the client (Sec. 15-10).

Sponsoring broker relationship. A sponsoring broker who appoints designated agents is not considered to be acting for more than one party as a dual agent if the licensees designated as legal agent of each client are not representing more than one party in the related transaction. The sponsoring broker has the contractual relationship with the client, and the designated agent has the agency relationship.

- **Confidentiality** A sponsoring broker who has appointed designated agents must protect confidential information disclosed by a client to his or her designated agent. This means the sponsoring broker must ensure that the only licensees accessing the client's records, including offers, contracts, financial information, or any other confidential information of the client are the client's designated agent(s) and the sponsoring broker.

Agency disclosure. Licensees must complete the agency disclosure to consumers in writing no later than the commencement of work as a designated agent. The disclosure expresses that a designated agency relationship exists. It may be included in the brokerage agreement or as a separate document.

BROKERAGE AGREEMENTS

A brokerage agreement is a written or oral agreement between a sponsoring broker and a consumer for licensed activities to be provided to the consumer for compensation or the right to receive compensation, and may be either a bilateral or unilateral agreement, depending on the agreement's content.

Exclusives. An exclusive brokerage agreement is an agreement that provides the sponsoring broker with the sole right, through one or more sponsored licensees, to act as the exclusive designated agent or representative of the client and meets the requirements as outlined in the Act.

Brokerage agreement requirements

In writing. Exclusive listing agreements and exclusive buyer brokerage agreements are agency agreements and must be in writing.

Minimal services. Exclusive agreements must include the required minimal services to be provided by the sponsoring broker through one or more sponsored licensees. Failing to include the minimal services or language waiving those services will result in the brokerage agreement being considered non-exclusive (Sec.15-75; 1450.770).

The required minimal services to be stated in all exclusive agreements are

- accept delivery of and present to the client offers and counteroffers to buy, sell, or lease the client's property or property the client seeks to purchase or lease
- assist the client in developing, communicating, negotiating, and presenting offers, counteroffers, and notices that relate to the offers and counteroffers until a lease or purchase agreement is signed and all contingencies are satisfied or waived
- answer the client's questions relating to the offers, counteroffers, notices, and contingencies

Required contents of agreements. Written brokerage agreements (buyer brokerage agreements and listing agreements), both exclusive and non-exclusive, must contain

- basis or amount of compensation and time of payment
- broker duties
- signature of sponsoring broker and client (or authorized agent)
- duration of brokerage agreement, or the client's right to terminate the agreement annually by giving no more than 30 days' prior written notice (if neither is included, the agreement will be considered void)
- statement that no amendment or alteration to terms regarding commission and time of payment will be valid unless made in writing and signed by the parties
- statement that it is illegal for the owner or licensee to refuse to show, display, lease, or sell to any person because of membership in a protected class under the Illinois Human Rights Act

Written listing agreements must also contain a listing price and identification of the real property (address or legal description)

Duties after termination. The sponsoring broker and any affiliated licensee owes only two duties after termination, expiration or completion of the brokerage agreement:

- accounting for all money and property relating to the transaction
- keeping confidential all confidential information received during the brokerage agreement; the duty of confidentiality does not terminate (Sec. 15-30)

RESIDENTIAL PROPERTY CONDITION DISCLOSURE

Illinois require sellers to make a written disclosure about property condition to a prospective buyer. This seller disclosure may or may not relieve the agent of some liabilities for disclosure. The residential property condition disclosure is the seller's written summary of the property's condition at the time of contracting for sale. The disclosure is entered on state-approved forms.

Owner's role

State legislation requires owners of previously occupied single-family homes and buildings containing 1-4 dwelling units to provide the disclosure to prospective buyers if they are selling, exchanging, or optioning their property. Some exceptions and exemptions apply. When required, the disclosure must be transmitted to the prospective buyer no later than when the buyer makes an offer.

A typical form requires the seller to affirm whether or not problems exist in any of the listed features and systems of the property. In denying that a problem exists, the seller claims to have no knowledge of a defect. If a defect does in fact exist, the seller can be held liable for intentional misrepresentation. A third possible response to a property condition question is that of "no representation." Here, the seller makes no claim of knowledge as to whether a problem exists. With this answer, the seller is no longer held liable for a disclosure of any kind relating to a particular feature, whether a defect is known or otherwise.

Once the seller has signed the form and delivered it to the buyer, the buyer must acknowledge receipt and knowledge of the property condition disclosures, along with other provisions set forth on the form.

Licensee's role

The residential property re-seller must comply with the property condition disclosure requirement whether an agent is employed in the transaction or not. If an agent is involved in the transaction, the agent must disclose any and all material facts he or she knows or should reasonably know about the property, regardless of what the seller may have disclosed on the form.

Right of rescission

Sellers who fail to complete and deliver the property condition disclosure statement to buyers in a timely fashion effectively give the buyer a subsequent right under certain conditions to rescind the sale contract and re-claim their deposits. The buyer must follow certain procedures and meet certain deadlines in order to legitimately effect the cancellation. The buyer's right to cancel persists until closing or occupancy, whichever comes first.

Property condition and material facts

As explained earlier in this chapter, an agent has the duty to inform the client of all material facts, reports, and rumors that might affect the client's interests in the property transaction. A material fact is one that might affect the value or desirability of the property to a buyer if the buyer knew it. Material facts include

- the agent's opinion of the property's condition
- adverse facts about property condition, title defects, environmental hazards, and property defects

In recent years, the disclosure standard has been raised to require an agent to disclose items that a practicing agent should know, whether the agent actually had the knowledge or not, and regardless of whether the disclosure furthers or impedes the progress of the transaction.

Facts not considered to be material, and therefore not usually subject to required disclosure, include such items as property stigmatization (e.g., that a crime or death occurred on the property) and the presence of registered sex offenders in the neighborhood (in accordance with Megan's Law, federal legislation that requires convicted offenders to register with the state of residence; in some states, agents must provide registry information to buyers).

The agent may be held liable for failing to disclose a material fact if a court rules that the typical agent in that area would detect and recognize the adverse condition. There is no obligation to obtain or disclose information that is immaterial to the transaction, such as property stigmas.

An agent who sees a "red flag" issue such as a potential structural or mechanical problem should advise the seller to seek expert advice. Red flags can seriously impact the value of the property and/or the cost of remediation. In addition to property condition per se, they may include such things as

- environmental concerns
- property anomalies, such as over-sized or peculiarly shaped lot
- neighborhood issues
- poor construction
- signs of flooding
- poor floorplan
- adjacent property features

Environmental disclosure obligations and liabilities

Licensees are expected to be aware of environmental issues and to know where to look for professional help. They are not expected to have expert knowledge of environmental law nor of physical conditions in a property. Rather, they must treat potential environmental hazards in the same way that they treat other material facts about a property: disclosure. It is advisable to have an attorney draft the appropriate disclosures to lessen the broker's liability should problems occur in the future.

In summary, for their own protection, licensees should be careful to:

- be aware of potential hazards
- disclose known material facts
- distribute the HUD booklet
- know where to seek professional help.

WARRANTIES

Purpose and scope

Home warranties, or home service contracts, cover service, repair, or replacement of a home's major systems and appliances. Warranties are usually purchased for one year at a time with the annual cost determined by the following:

- the location of the property – prices vary from state to state due to cost of living and property regulations in the specific area
- the type of property – single family homes have different price points than mobile homes or multifamily properties
- the size of the property – smaller homes have cheaper coverage options than large homes. often, the home's square footage determines the cost of the warranty
- the amount of coverage – standard coverage plans may exclude certain parts of the property, resulting in a lower price for the plan. The excluded items can be covered with a more extensive plan at a higher cost

Home warranties are often included in the purchase price of a home or are purchased by the buyer at the time of the home purchase.

Limitations

Purchasers of home warranties need to fully understand their coverage limitations in order to have realistic expectations of the warranty. Similarly, it is important for a homeowner to understand what may not be covered in the warranty. These items may include

- conditions that existed prior to the effective coverage of the warranty
- failures caused by something other than normal wear and tear
- improperly installed or modified items
- damages caused by failure of another system or appliance, such as kitchen cabinets being damaged from a plumbing leak in the pipes under the sink, called consequential damages
- outdoor items such as sprinklers or swimming pool
- repairs to faucets
- refrigerators, washers and dryers, or garage door openers are often not covered

Basically, unless an item is specifically listed in the warranty contract, it will not be covered.

With a home warranty, the homeowner must go through the warranty company to have the service performed. The company usually has established relationships with specific service providers and may use only those providers for service under the warranty. The homeowner is typically charged a service fee on top of the annual fee for each repair job.

INSPECTIONS

Property inspections may identify builder oversights or the need for major repairs. They may also identify the need for regular maintenance to keep the property in good condition. In addition to looking for structural issues, plumbing and electrical problems, and roof and foundation issues, inspections can uncover termites or other pests that are damaging the structure. Inspections can also uncover environmental issues that have a detrimental impact on the property.

The 4 point inspection covers the major systems in a home (AC, roof, plumbing and electrical). This is the report that insurance companies review to determine an accurate insurance quote. If a home is newer (around 25 years old depending on the insurance company), then a 4 point inspection is not required.

A "wind mitigation" report determines whether the home is eligible for any home insurance discounts. The buyer may also order a full inspection which identifies very specific imperfections in a home. If a home has a septic, well, or pool it will also need additional inspections. Mobile/manufactured homes also require different inspections.

WDO/Termite inspections

Termites are destructive pests that exist in all states except Alaska. They cause an estimated $50 billion in damage to buildings each year. They often cause extensive damage to the property before the owner even realizes there is a problem. Having homes inspected annually for termites can prevent substantial damage and cost.

The most common type of termite is the subterranean termite. They are often confused with winged ants, but they are much more destructive. Termite inspectors look for the following indications that termites are present in the structure:

- swarms of termites inside the home

- termite excrement

- termite bodies found in spider webs near the structure

- long, deep grooves in wood

Because termites cause such extensive damage and can live inside the structure of a home for years, a termite inspection should be part of any home buying transaction as well as a periodic event.

Environmental inspections

Home inspections should include looking for common environmental issues that can affect the property and the residents of the property. Environmental hazards can have a significant impact on the sale of a property. An environmental site assessment (ESA) may be conducted to identify environmental impairments and protect parties against becoming involved in contamination issues. Such assessments are performed in three phases. A Phase 1 ESA identifies potential problems on or near the subject property. A Phase 2 ESA involves active testing of soil, water, and other components of the subject property.

Environmental impact statements

When a project is federally funded, the responsible parties must provide an environmental impact statement (EIS) detailing how the project will affect the environment. Privately funded projects are also often required to prepare an EIS before any permits are issued. An EIS is expected to address air and water quality issues, noise, health and safety, wildlife, vegetation, water and sewer requirements, traffic, population density, and other issues as appropriate.

Licensee disclosure duties

Most states require disclosure of known material facts regarding residential properties of one to four units. If a licensee knows the result of an inspection, this is a material fact to be disclosed. Disclosure of environmental issues on commercial and industrial properties is often not mandated. Where disclosure is not required, real estate licensees should suggest the use of a professional environmental audit.

===

Check Your Understanding Challenges:

Chapter Two: Agency and Disclosure Issues

Carefully read each question then provide your best answer based on what you learned in this chapter. Then check your answers against the Answer Key which immediately follows the chapter questions.

1. The licensee has an obligation to fulfill certain general duties for the client. One of these is to perform the terms of the brokerage agreement. Name three additional duties.

    1. _____

    2. _____

    3. _____

2. Illinois licensees are required to treat all customers honestly and not intentionally give them false information. In addition, they are owed two critical disclosures? What are they?

    Disclosure #1: _____

    Disclosure #2: _____

3. There are nine permitted activities of a dual agent mentioned in this chapter. Can you name five of them?

    1. _____

    2. _____

    3. _____

    4. _____

    5. _____

4. The purpose of designated agency is to enable the sponsoring broker to

    a. get compensated by both a buyer and a seller on a single transaction.

    b. avoid the confusion and conflict inherent in a dual agency relationship within the firm.

    c. identify what licensee is specifically entitled to a commission at closing.

    d. avoid having to create burdensome relationship agreements

5. The confidentiality standard is one of the duties that extend beyond the termination of the listing since at no time in the future may the agent disclose confidential information. **TRUE** or FALSE

Answer: _____

6. Illinois agency law incorporated the concept of "minimum services" into its brokerage agreement requirements. This means that, to be an exclusive agreement, the client must receive the minimum services by sponsored licensees in the firm. In your own words, what are the three minimum services?

1. _____

_____

2. _____

_____

3. _____

_____

7. In the course of a transaction, the residential property condition disclosure must be completed and properly disseminated to buyer prospects. In a couple of sentences, distinguish the between the role of the seller and the role of the licensee in fulfilling this disclosure requirement.

Seller's role: _____

_____

_____

Licensee's role: _____

_____

_____

Answer Key: Check Your Understanding Challenges

Chapter Two: Agency and Disclosure Issues

1. The licensee has an obligation to fulfill certain general duties for the client. One of these is to perform the terms of the brokerage agreement. Name three additional duties.

   1. **promote the client's best interests**

   2. **exercise reasonable skill and care in performing services**

   3. **maintain confidentiality regarding client-received information**

2. Illinois licensees are required to treat all customers honestly and not intentionally give them false information. In addition, they are owed two critical disclosures? What are they?

   Disclosure #1:   Agency disclosure completed prior to receiving confidential information – that the agent is not working as the customer's agent

   Disclosure #2:   Property condition: must disclose all known material adverse facts regarding the physical condition of the property.

3. There are nine permitted activities of a dual agent mentioned in this chapter. Can you name five of them?

   - **Treat all clients honestly.**
   - **Provide information about the property to the buyer or tenant.**
   - **Disclose all latent material defects of the property that are known to the licensee.**
   - **Disclose financial qualifications of the buyer or tenant to the seller or landlord.**
   - **Explain real estate terms.**
   - **Help the buyer or tenant arrange for property inspections.**
   - **Explain closing costs and procedures.**
   - **Help the buyer compare financing options.**
   - **Provide information about comparable properties that have sold so both clients may make educated decisions on what price to accept or offer.**

4. The purpose of designated agency is to enable the sponsoring broker to

   b. avoid the confusion and conflicts of interest inherent in a dual agency relationship within the firm.

5. The confidentiality standard is one of the duties that extend beyond the termination of the listing since at no time in the future may the agent disclose confidential information.

Answer: True. **The duty of client confidentiality survives the listing agreement's term, as well as closing.**

6. What are the three minimum services?

1. accept and present offers to buy, sell or lease

2. assist in developing, communicating, negotiating and presenting offers and notices until sales contract or lease is signed and all contingencies are satisfied or waived.

3. answer client questions relating to offers, counters, notices and contingencies'

7. In the course of a transaction, the residential property condition disclosure must be completed and properly disseminated to buyer prospects. In a couple of sentences, distinguish the between the role of the seller and the role of the licensee in fulfilling this disclosure requirement.

Seller's role: Seller is primarily responsible for completing the disclosure whether using a broker or not. The report must be given to the buyer prior to making an offer. Seller may claim no knowledge of a given property condition factor.

Licensee's role: The licensee should advise the seller of the completion requirement. He or she must also disclose any known material facts regardless of seller's disclosures.

Interactive Exercises

Chapter 2: Agency and Disclosure Issues

ROLE PLAY SITUATIONAL CASE STUDY 5: Designated agency disclosure/dual agency

Coty has a successful listing presentation and lands a listing! A few days later, he hosts an open house for the listing to garner traffic and in walks Allie, an un-represented buyer. It is every agent's dream to sell their own listing at an open house to an un-represented buyer! Despite that being the goal, it is virtually unheard of but Coty gets lucky.

Allie walks through the property and immediately falls in love. Coty rushes to tell his sellers about his successful open houses and types up an offer for Allie. Before presenting the offer he discloses to his sellers that he is representing Allie.

Did Coty do anything wrong? After all, he did disclose the relationship to his sellers.

_____

_____

_____

_____

_____

_____

_____

_____

_____

_____

Case Debrief:

First of all, it is unclear whether Allie understood that Coty was the listing agent and represented the sellers. Oftentimes, open houses are hosted by colleagues of the listing agent. Allie could have been under the impression that Coty did not represent the sellers.

When participating in dual agency, the agent has to inform all parties of his obligations and duties. Not only that, but a verbal disclosure is not sufficient. Coty must receive written consent and confirmation from each party.

Next time Coty encounters a situation like this, he should immediately present all parties with a dual agency agreement, explain what it means for them, and receive their written consent.

===

"WHAT IF" SITUATIONAL EXAMPLE 1: Distressed property issues

David is working with an investor client, Abby, and she is curious about a few distressed properties in her neighborhood. One of them is a duplex in foreclosure and has water damaged floors from a roof leak, another is a single family home that has structural foundation issues, and the last one is a condominium with mold damage.

They each have unique issues and Abby asks David for his advice on each property. Which is the better investment?

David has a few contractors come out to each property and estimate the repair work that needs to be done and here's what he finds out:

Option	Property Type	Damages	Repair Cost
A	Duplex	Damaged floors & roof leak	$15,000
B	SFH	Foundation issues	$20,000
C	Condo	Mold issues	$10,000

So which property should David suggest? What else does he need to find out to help Abby make an informed decision?

_____

_____

_____

_____

_____

_____

_____

_____

_____

Case Debrief:

Before coming to any conclusion, David first needs to ask Abby what she plans to do with the properties. Is she looking to renovate and sell them or keep them as rentals? If she plans on renting them out then David needs to help her determine what the average rental cost is and what her capitalization rate would be for the homes. If Abby decides to just flip the homes, he will need to determine what the "After Repair Value" of the properties is so she can determine where she would profit the most.

Another thing to note is that if Abby plans to rent out the duplex, they have to figure out why it is in foreclosure. Typically, that means the rent is not profitable enough to help maintain the property so it might not be the best option for an investor. Sometimes subtle information like this is easily overlooked by clients, so David can help Abby with his experience.

At the end of the day, David has to present every material fact to Abby and let her make her own informed decision.

===

"WHAT IF" SITUATION EXAMPLE 2: Inspection/repairs issues

Richard is under contract on a home and after having an inspection done he is overwhelmed and does not know what repairs to request from the sellers. Should he ask them to fix all of the screens on the windows? Upgrade the windows to double pane? Or should he focus on the electrical issues? That's where his agent, William comes into play.

William walks Richard through the inspection report and helps him make sense of the inspector's mumbo-jumbo.

Which repairs should Richard and William try to negotiate?

_____

_____

_____

_____

_____

_____

_____

_____

_____

Case Debrief:

When William walks through the inspection report, he should explain to Richard that in a seller's market, the sellers hold more negotiating power. The most important items to focus on are those that insurance would have an issue with. Since the four-point inspection report is submitted to the insurance companies, that is the report that should be combed through to determine the negotiating points.

The four-point inspection calls out issues with the roof, electrical and plumbing systems, and HVAC system. These are the items that absolutely need to get fixed in order to obtain insurance, and in turn, financing. Everything else is just the "cherry on top" and if Richard decides he would like William to negotiate for all of the items then it is William's duty to oblige and fight for his client.

In this particular situation, albeit costly, the windows and screens would not be four-point issues. Thus, they are not deemed "necessary" by insurance companies. The electrical issues would need to be fixed in order to find acceptable insurance so those are the top priority in the repair negotiations.

===

CHAPTER 3:

FAIR HOUSING, ANTITRUST, AND OTHER ANTI-DISCRIMINATION LAWS

Chapter Three Learning Objectives: When the student has completed this chapter he or she will be able to:

- Summarize the purpose and thrust of the Illinois Human Rights Act
- Define and describe the principal forms of illegal discrimination
- Identify what parties are exempt from the fair housing prohibitions
- Describe how fair housing violations are enforced
- Summarize the key provisions of the Americans with Disabilities Act
- Define and summarize the principal forms of anti-trust legislation, including The Sherman Antitrust Act, Clayton Antitrust Act, collusion; price fixing; market allocation; and tie-in agreements

Federal and state governments have enacted laws prohibiting discrimination in the national housing market. The aim of these fair housing laws, or equal opportunity housing laws, is to give all people in the country an equal opportunity to live wherever they wish, provided they can afford to do so, without impediments of discrimination in the purchase, sale, rental, or financing of property.

STATE FAIR HOUSING LAWS

Federal and state governments have enacted laws prohibiting discrimination in the national housing market. The aim of these fair housing laws, or equal opportunity housing laws, is to give all people in the country an equal opportunity to live wherever they wish, provided they can afford to do so, without impediments of discrimination in the purchase, sale, rental, or financing of property.

Fair housing and local zoning

The Fair Housing Act prohibits a broad range of practices that discriminate against individuals on the basis of race, color, religion, sex, national origin, familial status, and disability. The Act does not pre-empt local zoning laws. However, the Act applies to municipalities and other local government entities and prohibits them from making zoning or land use decisions or implementing land use policies that exclude or otherwise discriminate against protected persons, including individuals with disabilities.

Illinois Human Rights Act (775 ILCS 5)

The Illinois Human Rights Act prohibits discrimination in housing based upon *race, color, religion, sex, pregnancy, national origin, ancestry, age, order of protection status, marital status, sexual orientation, unfavorable military discharge, physical and mental disability, and familial status.*

Discrimination is a license law violation as well as a crime, and can result in disciplinary action including loss of license, criminal prosecution and a lawsuit.

When a licensee is found guilty in a civil or criminal proceeding of illegal discrimination while performing real estate activity, the Department, upon recommendation of the Board, will suspend or revoke the licensee's license in a timely manner, unless the case is in the appeal process (Sec. 20-50).

FORMS OF ILLEGAL DISCRIMINATION

The Fair Housing Act specifically prohibits such activities in residential brokerage and financing as the following.

Discriminatory misrepresentation

An agent may not conceal available properties, represent that they are not for sale or rent, or change the sale terms for the purpose of discriminating. For example, an agent may not inform a minority buyer that the seller has recently decided not to carry back second mortgage financing when in fact the owner has made no such decision.

Discriminatory advertising

An agent may not advertise residential properties in such a way as to restrict their availability to any prospective buyer or tenant.

Providing unequal services

An agent may not alter the nature or quality of brokerage services to any party based on race, color, sex, national origin, or religion. For example, if it is customary for an agent to show a customer the latest MLS publication, the agent may not refuse to show it to any party. Similarly, if it is customary to show qualified buyers prospective properties immediately, an agent may not alter that practice for purposes of discrimination.

Steering

Steering is the practice of directly or indirectly channeling customers toward or away from homes and neighborhoods. Broadly interpreted, steering occurs if an agent describes an area in a subjective way for the purpose of encouraging or discouraging a buyer about the suitability of the area.

For example, an agent tells Buyer A that a neighborhood is extremely attractive, and that desirable families are moving in every week. The next day, the agent tells Buyer B that the same neighborhood is deteriorating, and that values are starting to fall. The agent has blatantly steered Buyer B away from the area and Buyer A into it.

Blockbusting

Blockbusting is the practice of inducing owners in an area to sell or rent to avoid an impending change in the ethnic or social makeup of the neighborhood that will cause values to go down.

For example, Agent Smith tells neighborhood owners that several minority families are moving in, and that they will be bringing their relatives next year. Smith informs homeowners that, in anticipation of a value decline, several families have already made plans to move.

Restricting MLS participation. It is discriminatory to restrict participation in any multiple listing service based on one's race, religion, national origin, color, or sex.

Redlining

Redlining is the residential financing practice of refusing to make loans on properties in a certain neighborhood regardless of a mortgagor's qualifications. In effect, the lender draws a red line around an area on the map and denies all financing to applicants within the encircled area.

Specific violations. Specific instances of discriminatory violations in real estate practice include:

- refusing to engage in a real estate transaction with a person
- refusing to make a transaction available
- refusing to receive or transmit an offer
- refusing to negotiate a transaction
- altering the terms, conditions, or privileges in a real estate transaction
- furnishing unequal facilities or services regarding a transaction
- falsely representing that a property is not available for inspection, sale, rental or lease
- failing to bring a listing to a party's attention
- refusing to permit an individual to inspect a property
- indicating a preference, limitation or discrimination based on a protected class in any advertising, record, or inquiry
- offering, soliciting, accepting or using a real estate listing knowing that any discrimination is intended

TITLE VIII EXEMPTIONS

The Fair Housing Act allows for exemptions under a few specific circumstances. These are:

- sale by owner of a single-family home if the owner owns no more than three single family homes, the owner or family member was the last resident, the home is sold without use of a real estate licensee, and no discriminatory ads are used
- rental of housing of four units or less if owner resides in one of the units
- rental of rooms in a private home if owner or family member resides there, or intends to reside there after an absence of no more than twelve months
- local, state, or federal maximum occupancy standards
- religious organizations and not-for-profit groups in conjunction with religious organizations, if not run commercially
- rental of rooms in housing for persons of one sex

- housing for seniors

ANTI-DISCRIMINATION ENFORCEMENT

Discrimination by the client

Fair housing laws apply to home sellers as well as to agents, with the exception of the exemptions previously cited. If an agent goes along with a client's discriminatory act, the agent is equally liable for violation of fair housing laws. It is thus imperative to avoid complicity with client discrimination. Further, an agent should withdraw from any relationship where client discrimination occurs.

Examples of potential client discrimination are:

- refusing a full-price offer from a party
- removing the property from the market to sidestep a potential purchase by a party
- accepting an offer from one party that is lower than one from another party

Violations and enforcement

Persons who feel they have been discriminated against under federal fair housing laws may file a complaint with the Office of Fair Housing and Equal Opportunity (FHEO) within HUD, or they may file suit in a federal or state court.

Filing an FHEO complaint

Complaints alleging fair housing violations must be filed with the Office of Fair Housing and Equal Opportunity within one year of the violation. HUD then initiates an investigation in conjunction with federal or local enforcement authorities.

If HUD decides that the complaint merits further action, it will attempt to resolve the matter out of court. If efforts to resolve the problem fail, the aggrieved party may file suit in state or federal court.

Filing suit

In addition to or instead of filing a complaint with HUD, a party may file suit in state or federal court within two years of the alleged violation.

Penalties

If discrimination is confirmed in court, the respondent may be enjoined to cease practicing his or her business. For example, a discriminating home builder may be restrained from selling available properties to buyers. Also, the plaintiff may be compensated for damages including humiliation, suffering, and pain. In addition, the injured party may seek equitable relief, including forcing the guilty party to complete a denied action such as selling or renting the property. Finally, the courts may impose civil penalties for first-time or repeat offenders.

AMERICANS WITH DISABILITIES ACT

The ADA, which became law in 1990, is a civil rights law that prohibits discrimination against individuals with disabilities in all areas of public life, including employment, education, transportation, and facilities that are open to the general public. The purpose of the law is to make sure that people with disabilities have the same rights and opportunities as everyone else.

The Americans with Disabilities Act Amendments Act (ADAAA) became effective on January 1, 2009. Among other things, the ADAAA clarified that a disability is "a physical or mental impairment that substantially limits one or more major life activities." This definition applies to all titles of the ADA and covers private employers with 15 or more employees, state and local governments, employment agencies, labor unions, agents of the employer, joint management labor committees, and private entities considered places of public accommodation. Examples of the latter include hotels, restaurants, retail stores, doctor's offices, golf courses, private schools, day care centers, health clubs, sports stadiums, and movie theaters.

ADA Titles

The law consists of five parts:

- Title I (Employment) concerns equal employment opportunity. It is enforced by the U.S. Equal Employment Opportunity Commission.
- Title II (State and Local government) concerns nondiscrimination in state and local government services. It is enforced by the U.S. Department of Justice.
- Title III (Public Accommodations) concerns nondiscrimination in public accommodations and commercial facilities. It is enforced by the U.S. Department of Justice.
- Title IV (Telecommunications) concerns accommodations in telecommunications and public service messaging. It is enforced by the Federal Communications Commission.
- Title V (Miscellaneous) concerns a variety of general situations including how the ADA affects other laws, insurance providers, and lawyers.

Real estate practitioners are most likely to encounter Titles I and III and should acquire familiarity with these. In advising clients, licensees are well-advised to seek qualified legal counsel.

Accommodating access to facilities

The ADA also requires that disabled employees and members of the public be provided access that is equivalent to that provided to those who are not disabled.

- Employers with at least fifteen employees must follow nondiscriminatory employment and hiring practices.
- Reasonable accommodations must be made to enable disabled employees to perform essential functions of their jobs.
- Modifications to the physical components of a building may be necessary to provide the required access to tenants and their customers, such as widening doorways, changing door hardware, changing how doors open, installing ramps, lowering wall-mounted telephones and keypads, supplying Braille signage, and providing auditory signals.
- Existing barriers must be removed when the removal is "readily achievable," that is, when cost is not prohibitive. New construction and remodeling must meet a higher standard.

- If a building or facility does not meet requirements, the landlord must determine whether restructuring or retrofitting or some other kind of accommodation is most practical.

Violations

Violations of ADA requirements can result in citations, business license restrictions, fines, and injunctions requiring remediation of the offending conditions. Business owners may also be held liable for personal injury damages to an injured plaintiff.

ANTI-TRUST LAWS

Brokerage companies, like other businesses, are subject to anti-trust laws designed to prevent monopolies and unfair trade practices.

Sherman Antitrust Act

Enacted in 1890, the Sherman Antitrust Act prohibits restraint of interstate and foreign trade by conspiracy, monopolistic practice, and certain forms of business combinations, or mergers. The Sherman Act empowers the federal government to proceed against antitrust violators.

Clayton Antitrust Act

The Clayton Antitrust Act of 1914 reinforces and broadens the provisions of the Sherman Act. Among its prohibitions are certain exclusive contracts, predatory price cutting to eliminate competitors, and inter-related boards of directors and stock holdings between same-industry corporations. The Clayton Act also legalizes certain labor strikes, picketing, and boycotts.

The effect of antitrust legislation is to prohibit trade practice and trade restraints that unfairly disadvantage open competition. Business practices and behaviors which violate antitrust laws include collusion, price fixing, market allocation, bid rigging, restricting market entry, exclusive dealing, and predatory pricing.

Collusion

Collusion is the illegal practice of two or more businesses joining forces or making joint decisions which have the effect of putting another business at a competitive disadvantage. Businesses may not collude to fix prices, allocate markets, create monopolies, or otherwise interfere with free market operations.

Price fixing

Price fixing is the practice of two or more brokers agreeing to charge certain commission rates or fees for their services, regardless of market conditions or competitors. In essence, such pricing avoids and disturbs the dynamics of a free, open market.

For instance, the two largest brokerages in a market jointly decide to cut commission rates by 50% in order to draw clients away from competitors. The cut-rate pricing could destroy smaller agencies that lack the staying power of the large companies.

Market allocation

Market allocation is the practice of colluding to restrict competitive activity in portions of a market in exchange for a reciprocal restriction from a competitor: "we won't compete against you here if you won't compete against us there."

For example, Broker A agrees to trade only in single family re-sales, provided that Broker B agrees to focus exclusively on apartment rentals and condominium sales. The net effect is an illegally restricted market where collusion and monopoly supplant market forces.

Tie-in agreements

In a tie-in agreement, the sale of one product or performance of a service is tied to the sale of another, less desirable product or service. For instance, "I will sell you this car, but you have to hire my brother-in-law to drive it." Or, more likely, "I will list and sell your old home if you hire me to find you a new home to purchase." Tie-ins restrict competition and limit the freedom of the consumer.

Violations of fair trade and anti-trust laws may be treated as felonies, and penalties can be substantial. Loss of one's license is also at stake. Brokers are well-advised to understand and recognize these laws.

Check Your Understanding Challenges:

Chapter Three: Fair Housing, Anti-Trust, and Other Anti-discrimination Laws

Carefully read each question then provide your best answer based on what you learned in this chapter. Then check your answers against the Answer Key which immediately follows the chapter questions.

1. An agent may not conceal available properties, represent that they are not for sale or rent, or change the sale terms for the purpose of discriminating. These prohibitions apply to 14 protected classes according to the Illinois Human Rights Act. Name ten of them by filling in the blanks which follow.

1. _____   6. _____

2. _____   7. _____

3. _____   8. _____

4. _____   9. _____

5. _____   10. _____

2. The text presents six general categories of illegal discrimination, for example, redlining. Name four of the five remaining types of discrimination and a single phrase definition of each type.

1. _____. Definition: _____

_____

2. _____. Definition: _____

_____

3. _____. Definition: _____

_____

4. _____. Definition: _____

_____

3. Which of the following is an example of an advertisement that violates the Fair Housing Act?

    a. Large home, perfect for large family
    b. Located in nice quiet neighborhood
    c. Located near shopping centers
    d. Many amenities nearby

4. Which of the following is legitimately exempt from anti-discrimination laws in Illinois?

    a. Housing for seniors
    b. Rental of housing of four units or less if the owner is over 55 years of age
    c. Rental of rooms in a private home
    d. Rental of housing units with leases in excess of one year

5. If a licensee goes along with a client's discriminatory act, the agent is equally liable for violation of fair housing laws. Is this true or false?

Answer: _____

6. Provide three examples of potential discrimination that a client might commit:

    1. _____
    2. _____
    3. _____

7. Persons who feel they have been discriminated against under federal fair housing laws may file a complaint with the _____ within HUD, or they may file suit in a federal or state court.

8. According to ADA, modifications to the physical components of a building are never required to be made by the owner of the building. TRUE or FALSE

Answer: _____

9. The two largest brokerages in a market jointly decide to cut commission rates to attract more clients. This is an example of

    a. Collusion
    b. Tie in agreement
    c. Price fixing
    d. Group boycotting

Answer Key: Check Your Understanding Challenges

Chapter Three: Fair Housing, Anti-Trust, and Other Anti-Discrimination Laws

1. Illinois protected classes:

   race   color   religion   sex

   pregnancy   national origin   ancestry   age

   order of protection status   marital status   sexual orientation

   unfavorable military discharge   physical and mental disability

   familial status

2. The five remaining types of discrimination are:

   1. **discriminatory misrepresentation: obstructing a transaction through false statements that are discriminatory**

   2. **discriminatory advertising: performing discriminatory acts in the process of advertising properties or oneself.**

   3. **providing unequal services: offering varying levels of service to different classes of customer that reflects a pattern of discrimination**

   4. **steering: channeling customers to or away from certain neighborhoods based on a discriminatory criteria**

   5. **blockbusting: inducing residents to sell based on an impending adverse change in the neighborhood's ethnic or social makeup.**

3. Which of the following is an example of an advertisement that violates the Fair Housing Act?

   A. **Large home, perfect for large family**

   A valuable guideline for writing non-discriminatory advertising copy: focus on the attributes of the property, not the residents.

4. Which of the following is legitimately exempt from anti-discrimination laws in Illinois?

   A. Housing for seniors

5. If a licensee goes along with a client's discriminatory act, the agent is equally liable for violation of fair housing laws. Is this true or false?

   Answer: **True**

6. Provide three examples of potential client discrimination:

- **refusing a full-price offer from a party**

- **removing the property from the market to sidestep a potential purchase by a party**

- **accepting an offer from one party that is lower than one from another party**

7. Persons who feel they have been discriminated against under federal fair housing laws may file a complaint with the **Office of Fair Housing and Equal Opportunity (FHEO**) within HUD, or they may file suit in a federal or state court.

8. According to ADA, modifications to the physical components of a building are never required to be made by the owner of the building.

> Answer: **FALSE; modifications may be required if they are reasonable and affordable. If an accommodation is prohibitively costly – such as widening all doorways – it does not have to be made.**

9. The two largest brokerages in a market jointly decide to cut commission rates to attract more clients. This is an example of

> **c. Price fixing**

===

Interactive Exercises

Chapter 3: Fair Housing, Anti-Trust, & Other Anti-Discrimination Laws

"WHAT IF" SITUATION EXAMPLE 3: Confronting Fair Housing violations/seller or buyer handling of failing contracts

As Olivia is running her morning MLS searches for clients, she notices that a new listing pops up in her neighborhood. It matches the exact criteria that her client Jamie has presented her but she doesn't want him to live in the neighborhood. She does not think he will fit in with the other neighbors and so avoids sending him the listing.

Later on, Jamie notices the listing when he looks online and asks Olivia to see it. Olivia makes up an excuse and says there is already a pending offer. A few days go by and the home is still marked active so Jamie calls the listing agent, sees the home and submits an offer without Olivia's help.

What would you do if you were Jamie?

Case Debrief:

_____

_____

_____

_____

_____

_____

_____

_____

_____

Jamie should conduct some research and find out whether Olivia violated any laws. After completing the due diligence, he would discover that Olivia violated the Fair Housing Act by deliberately failing to bring a listing to his attention. He can now file a complaint with her brokerage so she receives the appropriate disciplinary actions.

==

"WHAT IF" SITUATION EXAMPLE 4: Fair Housing questions

Mallory has been getting many calls on her current listing with questions about the home, neighborhood, etc. She was used to answering these common questions but last Wednesday she got a voicemail from a man named Chase who asked about the demographics in the neighborhood. He wanted to know what races lived in the area and whether or not it was a predominantly white neighborhood. His top priority was living in a suburb that has a high white population.

He also let it be known that he is an all cash buyer and would submit a proof of funds to her as soon as he got home.

How should Mallory approach the situation? What should she say to Chase?

_____

_____

_____

_____

_____

_____

_____

_____

_____

_____

Case Debrief:

Federal and state governments have enacted laws prohibiting discrimination in the national housing market. The aim of these fair housing laws, or equal opportunity housing laws, is to give all people in the country an equal opportunity to live wherever they wish, provided they can afford to do so, without impediments of discrimination in the purchase, sale, rental, or financing of property. One of the protected classes under the Fair Housing Act is race. Since it is a protected class Mallory cannot risk answering Chase's questions.

So what should she do? One way to tackle this situation is to urge Chase to complete his own due diligence by running online searches on demographics for the local neighborhood. There is lots of market data available online and Chase can discover the answers for himself without putting Mallory's license at risk.

===

"WHAT IF" SITUATION EXAMPLE 5: Anti-trust scenarios

Quintin and Samantha were talking by the water cooler at their office one day about a listing appointment they were going on that afternoon. After a few minutes they both realized they were heading to the same appointment! They knew the sellers were only interviewing two agents so it was helpful knowing who the competition was. They decided it was only fair if the sellers chose them based on their qualifications and not on a discounted commission so they promised each other they would both charge a 6% listing fee and would not budge no matter what. This way, the appointments would be fair.

What do you think? Is their thinking along the right lines?

_____

_____

_____

_____

_____

_____

_____

_____

_____

Case Debrief:

According to anti-trust laws, discussing commission can lead to a violation. Price fixing is the practice of two or more brokers agreeing to charge certain commission rates or fees for their services, regardless of market conditions or competitors. In essence, such pricing avoids and disturbs the dynamics of a free, open market. By promising to charge the exact same commission, Quintin and Samantha are actually involved in price fixing and violating anti-trust laws. They should not have discussed their commissions with each other and dropped the subject of the listing appointment as soon as they discovered they were both fighting for the same deal.

===

CHAPTER 4:
SALES CONTRACTS AND TRUST FUNDS

Chapter Four Learning Objectives: When the student has completed this chapter he or she will be able to:

- Define numerous legal characteristics of contract and sales contracts in particular, including validity; who may complete; contingencies; default; contract creation; and blank contracts
- Enumerate the essential requirements for compliant handling of trust fund deposits
- Summarize the various requirements for managing trust fund accounts
- List ways brokers can handle trust fund disputes and disputed disbursements
- Define the trust fund prohibitions of commingling and conversion
- Define and describe primary and secondary provisions of the sales contract

The conventional transfer of real estate ownership takes place in three stages. First, there is the negotiating period where buyers and sellers exchange offers in an effort to agree to all transfer terms that will appear in the sale contract. Second, when both parties have accepted all terms, the offer becomes a binding sale contract and the transaction enters the pre-closing stage, during which each party makes arrangements to complete the sale according to the sale contract's terms. Third is the closing of the transaction, when the seller deeds title to the buyer, the buyer pays the purchase price, and all necessary documents are completed. At this stage, the sale contract has served its purpose and terminates.

In Illinois, a real estate form intended to become a binding sales contract must state "Real Estate Sales Contract" in bold type at the top of the form.

LEGAL CHARACTERISTICS OF SALES CONTRACTS

Executory contract

A sale contract is executory: the signatories have yet to perform their respective obligations and promises. Upon closing, the sale contract is fully performed and no longer exists as a binding agreement.

Signatures

All owners of the property should sign the sale contract. If the sellers are married, both spouses should sign to ensure that both spouses release homestead rights to the buyer at closing. Failure to do so does not invalidate the contract but can lead to encumbered title and legal disputes.

Validity and enforceability

To be enforceable, a sale contract must:

- be validly created (mutual consent, consideration, legal purpose, competent parties, voluntary act)
- be in writing
- identify the principal parties
- clearly identify the property, preferably by legal description
- contain a purchase price
- be signed by the principal parties

The Illinois Statute of Frauds (740 ILCS 80/2) requires that the following contracts be in writing to be enforceable in court:

- contracts for the sale of real property
- leases longer than one year

A contract for the sale of real estate is enforceable only if it is in writing. A buyer or seller cannot sue to force the other to comply with an oral contract for sale, even if the contract is valid.

Assignment

Either party to a sale transaction can assign the sale contract to another party, subject to the provisions and conditions contained in the agreement.

Who may complete a sales contract?

A broker may assist buyer and seller in completing an offer to purchase. It is advisable, and legally required in most states, for a broker to use a standard contract form promulgated by state agencies or real estate boards, as such forms contain generally accepted language. This relieves the broker of the dangers of creating new contract language, which can be construed as a practice of law for which the broker is not licensed.

Real estate licensees may fill in the blanks on contract forms customarily used in the area if the forms have been prepared by an attorney.

Unauthorized practice of law

Real estate licensee drafting of contracts, riders, or addenda to contracts constitutes the unauthorized practice of law as determined by the Illinois Supreme Court decision in Chicago Bar Association, et al., v. Quinlan and Tyson, Inc.

Licensees are prohibited from preparing any legal document regarding the transaction, such as deed, title, or mortgage documents; conducting real estate closings; and providing legal advice. Offers to purchase, listing agreements, and addenda should be prepared by the local association as approved by an attorney.

Signing blank contracts. Licensees are prohibited from having a party sign a contract with blanks to be completed later. Changes or deletions in a contract should be only made at the direction of the party signing the contract and must be initialed or signed and dated. A licensee should advise a party who is unsure regarding any legal issue or language to use in adding information to a contract to contact an attorney.

Contract contingencies

A sale contract often contains contingencies. A contingency is a condition that must be met before the contract is enforceable.

The most common contingency concerns financing. A buyer makes an offer contingent upon securing financing for the property under certain terms on or before a certain date. If unable to secure the specified loan commitment by the deadline, the buyer may cancel the contract and recover the deposit. An appropriate and timely loan commitment eliminates the contingency, and the buyer must proceed with the purchase.

It is possible for both buyers and sellers to abuse contingencies in order to leave themselves a convenient way to cancel without defaulting. To avoid problems, the statement of a contingency should:

- be explicit and clear
- have an expiration date
- expressly require diligence in the effort to fulfill the requirement

A contingency that is too broad, vague, or excessive in duration may invalidate the entire contract on the grounds of insufficiency of mutual agreement.

Default

A sale contract is bilateral, since both parties promise to perform. As a result, either party may default by failing to perform. Note that a party's failure to meet a contingency does not constitute default, but rather entitles the parties to cancel the contract.

Buyer default. If a buyer fails to perform under the terms of a sale contract, the breach entitles the seller to legal recourse for damages. In most cases, the contract itself stipulates the seller's remedies. The usual remedy is forfeiture of the buyer's deposit as liquidated damages, provided the deposit is not grossly in excess of the seller's actual damages. It is also customary to provide for the seller and broker to share the liquidated damages. The broker may not, however, receive liquidated damages in excess of what the commission would have been on the full listing price.

If the contract does not provide for liquidated damages, the seller may sue for damages, cancellation, or specific performance.

Seller default. If a seller defaults, the buyer may sue for specific performance, damages, or cancellation.

Contract creation

Offer and acceptance.   A contract of sale is created by full and unequivocal acceptance of an offer. Offer and acceptance may come from either buyer or seller. The offeree must accept the offer without making any changes whatsoever. A change terminates the offer and creates a new offer, or counteroffer. An offeror may revoke an offer for any reason prior to communication of acceptance by the offeree.

Equitable title.   A sale contract gives the buyer an interest in the property that is called equitable title, or ownership in equity. If the seller defaults and the buyer can show good faith performance, the buyer can sue for specific performance, that is, to compel the seller to transfer legal title upon payment of the contract price.

TRUST FUND HANDLING

Trust account management

State laws prescribe how licensees must handle any escrow or earnest money deposits they receive. Those laws usually state that a broker must hold money received in connection with the purchase or lease of real property in a trust fund account. The type of account and financial depository are specified. The broker must record receipt of the money and place that money in the trust account within a specified time period. Usually, the law allows the broker to hold an earnest money check uncashed until the offer is accepted, provided the buyer gives written permission and the seller is informed.

Typical trust fund account management requirements include:

- the broker named as trustee of the account
- a federally-insured bank or recognized depository located in the state
- an account that is not interest-bearing if the financial institution ever requires prior written notice for withdrawals
- maintenance of records in a particular accounting format
- separate records kept for each beneficiary, property, or transaction
- records of funds received and paid out regularly reconciled with bank statements
- withdrawals only by the broker-trustee or other specifically authorized person

The buyer's earnest money deposit fulfills the consideration requirements for a valid sale contract. In addition, it provides potential compensation for damages to the seller if the buyer fails to perform. The amount of the deposit varies according to local custom. It should be noted that the earnest money deposit is not the only form of consideration that satisfies the requirement.

The sale contract provides the escrow instructions for handling and disbursing escrow funds. The earnest money is placed in a third-party trust account or escrow. A licensed escrow agent employed by a title company, financial institution, or brokerage company usually manages the escrow. An individual broker may also serve as the escrow agent.

The escrow holder acts as an impartial fiduciary for buyer and seller. If the buyer performs under the sale contract, the deposit is applied to the purchase price.

Strict rules govern the handling of earnest money deposits, particularly if a broker is the escrow agent. For example, state laws direct the broker when to deposit the funds, how to account for them, and how to keep them separate from the broker's own funds.

Rental security deposits

Rental security deposits must be placed into a non-interest bearing escrow account, with one exception: where a licensee is managing properties of 25 or more residential units, in a single building or in a complex located on contiguous parcels, and where security deposits are held for more than six months. In this case, interest must be paid to the lessees from the date of deposit. The interest is computed at the rate paid by the largest commercial bank in the state on minimum deposit passbook savings accounts as of December 31 of the calendar year immediately preceding the beginning of the rental agreement. Interest must be paid within 30 days after the end of each twelve-month period. This is an Illinois law requirement; however, some communities have stricter interest-payment requirements

Deposits

Escrow funds include earnest money, security deposits, promissory notes or other legal tender or financial consideration deposited for the benefit of the parties to a transaction, whether personal or cashier's checks, money orders, cash or other legal tender. An exception is a security deposit held by the sole owner of the property. Rent money paid to a licensee to be transmitted to the owner is not considered escrow funds. The sponsoring broker must provide a receipt to the payor of escrow funds and retain a copy (Sec. 20-20, 1450-750).

Sponsoring brokers are not required to maintain an escrow account if they do not accept escrow funds. Sponsoring brokers who accept escrow money must maintain and deposit the money into a special escrow account, separate from personal or other business accounts, in a federally insured depository, and may have more than one account.

Escrow money accepted by a sponsoring broker must be placed in the escrow account no later than the next business day following the transaction or after receipt, based on the terms of the contract. Funds received on a day prior to a bank holiday, or other day when the bank is closed, must be deposited on the next business day the depository is open.

The sponsoring broker is required to notify all principals in writing if a principal fails to provide escrow moneys, if a principal's payment is dishonored by the financial institution, or if, based on the contract, the amount of escrow money deposited is insufficient.

Withdrawals and disbursements

Earnest money must be kept in the account until a transaction is consummated or terminated once the payor's financial institution honors the deposit of the funds. The actual terms of the contract regarding release of the funds must be adhered to by the sponsoring broker. The funds may also be disbursed at the written direction of all parties.

If the sponsoring broker receives an order from a court providing for disbursement, the sponsoring broker must disburse escrow funds according to the court order.

Broker-owned funds

Commissions and fees earned by the sponsoring broker must be disbursed from the account no earlier than the day the transaction is consummated or terminated and no later than the next business day, or according to the written direction of the principals. Brokers may not withhold escrow funds because of a claim for commission or compensation.

Funds other than commissions and other funds owed to the broker may be transferred to the closing agent up to two business days prior to the scheduled closing.

Disputed or abandoned funds

In a dispute over earnest money, or if the broker is aware that a party contests the planned disbursement, the sponsoring broker must hold the deposit until a written release is received from all parties or their authorized agents, in which case the broker must release the funds by the next business day after receipt of the release.

If civil action is filed by the sponsoring broker or one of the parties to the transaction, the earnest money must be deposited with the court.

When six months have passed after receipt of a written demand for the disputed escrow money from one of the principals or the principal's authorized agent, and there is no resolution of the dispute and no notice of the filing of a claim in court, the funds may be considered abandoned and transferred to the State Treasurer.

After five years from the date of the parties' last indication of concern for the funds, they are deemed abandoned per the Revised Uniform Unclaimed Property Act and must be turned over to the State Treasurer.

Recordkeeping

Brokers must maintain a bookkeeping system that includes a journal showing chronological sequence of funds received and disbursed, a ledger for each transaction, a monthly bank statement, a master account log identifying all escrow accounts and banks holding accounts, and a monthly reconciliation statement that insures agreement between escrow account, journal and master escrow account log

Escrow records must be maintained for five years and backed up monthly, with the immediately prior two years' records being maintained in the sponsoring broker's office and produceable within 24 hours after a request by the Division. Records older than two years must be available for inspection within 30 days of the Division's request and may be stored off-site.

Any physical record required to be maintained must be securely stored and accessible to the Department at the sponsoring broker's principal office. Electronic records must be securely stored in the same format in which originally generated. Records must be backed up monthly.

Commingling and conversion in trust fund practices

Commingling is prohibited. The sponsoring broker must therefore deposit only escrow funds into an escrow account. The sponsoring broker may not deposit personal funds other than an amount sufficient to avoid service charges relating to the account. This amount must be specifically documented and may not exceed the minimum required to avoid incurring service charges.

Mixing of personal or company funds with client funds is grounds for the revocation or suspension of a real estate license. Depositing client funds in a personal or business account, or using them for any purpose other than the client's business, is also grounds for suspension or revocation of a license. It is important for the broker to remove commissions, fees or other income earned by the broker from a trust account within the period specified by law to avoid committing an act of commingling.

CONTRACT CONTINGENCIES

A sale contract often contains contingencies. A contingency is a condition that must be met before the contract is enforceable.

The most common contingency concerns financing. A buyer makes an offer contingent upon securing financing for the property under certain terms on or before a certain date. If unable to secure the specified loan commitment by the deadline, the buyer may cancel the contract and recover the deposit. An appropriate and timely loan commitment eliminates the contingency, and the buyer must proceed with the purchase.

It is possible for both buyers and sellers to abuse contingencies in order to leave themselves a convenient way to cancel without defaulting. To avoid problems, the statement of a contingency should:

- be explicit and clear
- have an expiration date
- expressly require diligence in the effort to fulfill the requirement

A contingency that is too broad, vague, or excessive in duration may invalidate the entire contract on the grounds of insufficiency of mutual agreement.

SALE CONTRACT PROVISIONS

Sale contracts can vary significantly in length and thoroughness. They also vary according to the type of sale transaction they describe. Some of the varieties are:

- Residential Contract of Sale
- Commercial Contract of Sale
- Foreclosure Contract of Sale
- Contract of Sale for New Construction
- Contract of Sale for Land
- Exchange Agreement

As the most common sale transaction is a residential sale, a Residential Contract of Sale is the type with which a licensee should first become familiar.

Primary provisions

The following provisions constitute the primary trusts of the sale contract.

Parties, consideration, and property. One or more clauses will identify the parties, the property, and the basic consideration, which is the sale of the property in return for a purchase price.

There must be at least two parties to a sale contract: one cannot convey property to oneself. All parties must be identified, be of legal age, and have the capacity to contract.

The property clause also identifies fixtures and personal property included in the sale. Unless expressly excluded, items commonly construed as fixtures are included in the sale. Similarly, items commonly considered personal property are not included unless expressly included.

Legal description. A legal description must be sufficient for a competent surveyor to identify the property.

Price and terms. A clause states the final price and details how the purchase will occur. Of particular interest to the seller is the buyer's down payment, since the greater the buyer's equity, the more likely the buyer will be able to secure financing. In addition, a large deposit represents a buyer's commitment to complete the sale.

If seller financing is involved, the sale contract sets forth the terms of the arrangement: the amount and type of loan, the rate and term, and how the loan will be paid off.

It is important for all parties to verify that the buyer's earnest money deposit, down payment, loan proceeds, and other promised funds together equal the purchase price stated in the contract.

Loan approval. A financing contingency clause states under what conditions the buyer can cancel the contract without default and receive a refund of the earnest money. If the buyer cannot secure the stated financing by the deadline, the parties may agree to extend the contingency by signing next to the changed dates.

Earnest money deposit. A clause specifies how the buyer will pay the earnest money. It may allow the buyer to pay it in installments. Such an option enables a buyer to hold on to the property briefly while obtaining the additional deposit funds. For example, a buyer who wants to buy a house makes an initial deposit of $200, to be followed in twenty-four hours with an additional $2,000. The sale contract includes the seller's acknowledgment of receipt of the deposit.

Escrow. An escrow clause provides for the custody and disbursement of the earnest money deposit, and releases the escrow agent from certain liabilities in the performance of escrow duties.

Closing and possession dates. The contract states when title will transfer, as well as when the buyer will take physical possession. Customarily, possession occurs on the date when the deed is recorded, unless the buyer has agreed to other arrangements.

The closing clause generally describes what must take place at closing to avoid default. A seller must provide clear and marketable title. A buyer must produce purchase funds. Failure to complete any pre-closing requirements stated in the sale contract is default and grounds for the aggrieved party to seek recourse.

Conveyed interest; type of deed. One or more provisions will state what type of deed the seller will use to convey the property, and what conditions the deed will be subject to. Among common "subject to" conditions are easements, association memberships, encumbrances, mortgages, liens, and special assessments. Typically, the seller conveys a fee simple interest by means of a general warranty deed.

Title evidence. The seller covenants to produce the best possible evidence of property ownership. This is commonly in the form of title insurance.

Damage and destruction.   A clause stipulates the obligations of the parties in case the property is damaged or destroyed. The parties may negotiate alternatives, including seller's obligation to repair, buyer's obligation to buy if repairs are made, and the option for either party to cancel.

Broker's representation and commission.

The broker discloses the applicable agency relationships in the transaction and names the party who must pay the brokerage commission.

Seller's representations.

The seller warrants that there will be no liens on the property that cannot be settled and extinguished at closing. In addition, the seller warrants that all representations are true, and if found otherwise, the buyer may cancel the contract and reclaim the deposit.

SECONDARY CONTRACT PROVISIONS

A sale contract may contain numerous additional clauses, depending on the complexity of the transaction. The following are some of the common provisions.

Inspections

The parties agree to inspections and remedial action based on findings.

Owner's association disclosure

The seller discloses existence of an association and the obligations it imposes.

Survey

The parties agree to a survey to satisfy financing requirements.

Environmental hazards

The seller notifies the buyer that there may be hazards that could affect the use and value of the property.

Compliance with laws

The seller warrants that there are no undisclosed building code or zoning violations.

Due-on-sale clause

The parties state their understanding that loans that survive the closing may be called due by the lender. Both parties agree to hold the other party harmless for the consequences of an acceleration.

Seller financing disclosure

The parties agree to comply with applicable state and local disclosure laws concerning seller financing.

Rental property; tenants rights

The buyer acknowledges the rights of tenants following closing.

FHA or VA financing condition

A contingency allows the buyer to cancel the contract if the price exceeds FHA or VA estimates of the property's value.

Flood plain; flood insurance

Seller discloses that the property is in a flood plain and that it must carry flood insurance if the buyer uses certain lenders for financing.

Condominium assessments

Seller discloses assessments the owner must pay.

Foreign seller withholding

The seller acknowledges that the buyer must withhold 15% of the purchase price at closing if the seller is a foreign person or entity and forward the withheld amount to the Internal Revenue Service. Certain limitations and exemptions apply.

Tax deferred exchange

For income properties only, buyer and seller disclose their intentions to participate in an exchange and agree to cooperate in completing necessary procedures.

Merger of agreements

Buyer and seller state that there are no other agreements

between the parties that are not expressed in the contract.

Notices

The parties agree on how they will give notice to each other and what they will consider to be delivery of notice.

Time is of the essence

The parties agree that they can amend dates and deadlines only if they both give written approval.

Fax transmission

The parties agree to accept facsimile transmission of the offer, provided receipt is acknowledged and original copies of the contract are subsequently delivered.

Survival

The parties continue to be liable for the truthfulness of representations and warranties after the closing.

Dispute resolution

The parties agree to resolve disputes through arbitration as opposed to court proceedings.

C.L.U.E. Report

CLUE (Comprehensive Loss Underwriting Exchange) is a claims history database used by insurance companies in underwriting or rating insurance policies. A CLUE Home Seller's Disclosure Report shows a five-year insurance loss history for a specific property. Among other things, it describes the types of any losses and the amounts paid. Many home buyers now require sellers to provide a CLUE Report (which only the property owner or an insurer can order) as a contingency appended to the purchase offer. A report showing a loss due to water damage and mold, for instance, might lead a buyer to decide against making an offer because of the potential difficulty of getting insurance. A report showing no insurance loss within the previous five years, on the other hand, is an indication that the availability and pricing of homeowner's insurance will not present an obstacle to the purchase transaction, and also that the property has not experienced significant damage or repair during that time period.

Addenda

Addenda to the sale contract become binding components of the overall agreement. The most common addendum is the seller's property condition disclosure. Examples of other addenda are:

- agency disclosure
- asbestos / hazardous materials
- radon disclosure
- liquidated damages
- flood plain disclosure
- tenant's lease

===

Check Your Understanding Challenges:

Chapter Four: Sales Contracts and Trust Funds

Carefully read each question then provide your best answer based on what you learned in this chapter. Then check your answers against the Answer Key which immediately follows the chapter questions.

1. The conventional transfer of real estate ownership can be grouped in three successive stages. Can you identify the three stages and their respective outcomes?

First
Stage:_____
_____
_____

Second
Stage:_____
_____
_____

Third
Stage:_____
_____
_____

2. A sale contract is considered to be a(n) _____ contract if the signatories have yet to perform their respective obligations and promises. (Complete the blank with your answer)

3. To be valid and enforceable, a sale contract must fulfill six criteria. Name four of these requirements:

1._____

2._____

3._____

4._____

4. In the context of a licensee completing legally binding contracts, which of the following is **FALSE**:

    a. Real estate licensees may fill in the blanks on contract forms customarily used in the area if the forms have been prepared by an attorney.

    b. Real estate licensee drafting of contracts, riders, or addenda to contracts constitutes the unauthorized practice of law.

    c. Real Estate licensees may prepare legal documents, such as deed, title, or mortgage documents if the client has authorized the licensee.

    d. Real estate licensees should use addenda that have been prepared by the local association as approved by an attorney.

5. Licensees are not prohibited from having a party sign a contract with blanks to be completed later.

    True or false?

6. A contract of sale is created by full and unequivocal _____ of an offer. Offer and acceptance may come from either buyer or seller. The _____ must accept the offer without making any changes whatsoever. A change _____ the offer and creates a new offer, or counteroffer. An _____ may revoke an offer for any reason prior to communication of acceptance by the offeree. (Fill in the blanks with your answers.)

7. Compliant trust fund account management carries with it numerous responsibilities or requirements. Name four of the requirements cited in the chapter narrative.

    1._____

    2._____

    3,_____

    4._____

8. Which of the following statements is TRUE regarding the handling and disbursement of escrow funds?

    a. Trust funds must be deposited in escrow no later than the next business day.
    b. The earnest money should always be placed in an interest nearing account.
    c. An individual broker may not serve as the escrow agent.
    d. The firm's policy manual establishes the escrow instructions for handling and disbursing escrow funds.

9. A real estate brokerage firm holding a transaction's escrow funds found itself in the middle of an earnest money dispute between the buyer and the seller. If no agreement is made as to how the trust money disbursement should be handled, how should the broker proceed if the broker no longer wants

to be the party responsible to continue to hold the earnest money? Describe in detail the action the broker should take.

Answer:

_____
_____
_____
_____
_____

10. Sales contract contingencies can be used in transactions to provide an "out" for either principal party. To reduce the occurrence of this adverse event, contingencies should be created according to several accepted guidelines. Name three of these guidelines as presented in the text.

1._____

2._____

3,_____

Answer Key: Check Your Understanding Challenges

Chapter Four: Sales Contracts and Trust Funds

1. The conventional transfer of real estate ownership can be grouped in three successive stages. Can you identify the three stages and their respective outcomes?

> **First stage: Negotiation. The negotiating period where buyers and sellers exchange offers in an effort to agree to all transfer terms that will appear in the sale contract.**

> **Second stage: Pre-closing. When both parties have accepted all terms, the offer becomes a binding sale contract, and the transaction enters the pre-closing stage. Here, each party makes arrangements to complete the sale according to the sale contract's terms.**

> **Third stage: Closing. The closing of the transaction is when the seller deeds title to the buyer, the buyer pays the purchase price, and all necessary documents are completed. At this stage, the sale contract has served its purpose and terminates.**

2. A sale contract is considered to be a(n) _____ contract if the signatories have yet to perform their respective obligations and promises. (Complete the blank with your answer)

> **executory**

3. To be valid and enforceable, a sale contract must fulfill six criteria. Name four of these requirements:

> **1. be validly created (has mutual consent, consideration, legal purpose, competent parties, is a voluntary act)**
> **2, be in writing**
> **3. identify the principal parties**
> **4. clearly identify the property, preferably by legal description**
> **5. contain a purchase price**
> **6..be signed by all principal parties**

4. In the context of a licensee completing legally binding contracts, which of the following is **FALSE**:

> **c. Real Estate licensees may prepare legal documents, such as deed, title, or mortgage documents if the client has authorized the licensee.**

5. Licensees are not prohibited from having a party sign a contract with blanks to be completed later.

> **False**

6. A contract of sale is created by full and unequivocal _____ of an offer. Offer and acceptance may come from either buyer or seller. The _____ must accept the offer

without making any changes whatsoever. A change _____ the offer and creates a new offer, or counteroffer. An _____ may revoke an offer for any reason prior to communication of acceptance by the offeree. (Fill in the blanks with your answers.)

acceptance; offeree; nullifies or cancels; offeror

7. Compliant trust fund account management carries with it numerous responsibilities or requirements. Name four of the requirements cited in the chapter narrative.

- **the sponsoring broker must be named as trustee of the account**
- **the account must be in a federally-insured bank or recognized depository located in the state**
- **the account cannot be interest-bearing if the financial institution ever requires prior written notice for withdrawals**
- **separate records must be kept for each beneficiary, property, or transaction**
- **the sponsoring broker must maintain records of funds received and paid out**
- **the account must be regularly reconciled with bank statements**
- **withdrawals may only be made by the specifically authorized person**

8. Which of the following statements is TRUE regarding the handling and disbursement of escrow funds?

a. Trust funds must be deposited in escrow no later than the next business day.

9 Describe in detail the action the broker should take to resolve his involvement in the escrow dispute.

When six months have passed after receipt of a written demand for the disputed escrow money from one of the principals, and there is no resolution of the dispute and no notice of the filing of a claim in court, the funds may be considered abandoned and transferred to the State Treasurer.

10. Sales contract contingencies can be used in transactions to provide an "out" for either principal party. To reduce the occurrence of this adverse event, contingencies should be created according to several accepted guidelines. Name three of these guidelines as presented in the text.

1. The contingency should be explicit and clear

2. The contingency should have an expiration date

3. The contingency should expressly require diligent effort to fulfill the condition.

==

Interactive Exercises

Chapter 4: Sales Contracts And Trust Funds

ROLE PLAY / SITUATIONAL CASE STUDY 6: Request writing purchase agreement/offer

As soon as Michael stepped into the house on Magnolia Ave, he immediately fell in love with the vaulted ceilings and farmhouse aesthetic. This was exactly what he was looking for and pictured. He could not believe that his dream home existed! Michael immediately told his Realtor, Jessica that he needed to submit an offer ASAP.

What does Jessica need in order to submit his offer?

_____

_____

_____

_____

_____

_____

_____

_____

_____

_____

Case Debrief:

Jessica will first need to call the listing agent to find out if there are any other offers. This will help determine what terms they should submit. After compiling a Comparative Market Analysis, Jessica can then discuss what the home is worth and allow Michael to make an informed decision about his offer price.

While he is deciding, Jessica will reach out to Michael's lender for an updated pre-approval letter. At this point he should have already gotten pre-approved, but if he hasn't then he needs to jump on that ASAP.

The other terms Jessica should also discuss with Michael is

    the length of the inspection period

    the escrow deposit amount

the closing date

the type of financing (conventional, VA, FHA, seller-financing, etc.

the amount of down-payment

any other special arrangements, contributions from the seller

what personal property is to be conveyed

Once she's gathered all of the information she will type up the offer and submit it with all of the necessary paperwork and notify the agent to look out for an incoming offer.

"WHAT IF" SITUATION EXAMPLE 6: Proper handling/disbursing escrow money

Sponsoring broker Annabelle is holding onto the escrow money for one of her real estate agents' current transactions, the listing agent on the deal. The listing agent is disputing the escrow deposit refund because she believes she is entitled to it since the buyers backed out after the inspection period. Since Annabelle believes her broker's story, she refuses to release it. The buyer's agent insists that they sent a cancellation form before the inspection period was over. Now the matter has turned into a full-blown escrow dispute.

How can Annabelle proceed? What should happen next?

_____

_____

_____

_____

_____

_____

_____

_____

_____

Case Debrief:

In a dispute over earnest money, or if the broker is aware that a party contests the planned disbursement, the sponsoring broker must hold the deposit until a written release is received from all parties or their authorized agents, in which case the broker must release the funds by the next business day after receipt of the release.

If civil action is filed by the sponsoring broker or one of the parties to the transaction, the earnest money must be deposited with the court.

When six months have passed after receipt of a written demand for the disputed escrow money from one of the principals or the principal's authorized agent, and there is no resolution of the dispute and no notice of the filing of a claim in court, the funds may be considered abandoned and transferred to the State Treasurer.

After five years from the date of the parties' last indication of concern for the funds, they are deemed abandoned per the Revised Uniform Unclaimed Property Act and must be turned over to the State Treasurer.

CHAPTER 5:
ESTIMATING MARKET VALUE

Chapter Five Learning Objectives: When the student has completed this chapter he or she will be able to:

- Define 'market value' and the pre-conditions for a valid market value estimate
- List the steps involved in the overall appraisal process encompassing the three approaches to value.
- Summarize the specific steps involved in generating a value estimate using the market data approach
- Identify how to complete a broker's comparative market analysis
- Describe the steps involved in the income approach to value

DEFINING MARKET VALUE

The valuation of real property is one of the most fundamental activities in the real estate business. Its role is particularly critical in the transfer of real property, since the value of a parcel establishes the general price range for the principal parties to negotiate.

Market value requirements

Market value is an opinion of the price that a willing seller and willing buyer would probably agree on for a property at a given time if:

- the transaction is a cash transaction
- the property is exposed on the open market for a reasonable period
- buyer and seller have full information about market conditions and about potential uses
- there is no abnormal pressure on either party to complete the transaction
- buyer and seller are not related (it is an "arm's length" transaction)
- title is marketable and conveyable by the seller
- the price is a "normal consideration," that is, it does not include hidden influences such as special financing deals, concessions, terms, services, fees, credits, costs, or other types of consideration.

Another way of describing market value is that it is the highest price that a buyer would pay and the lowest price that the seller would accept for the property.

The market price, as opposed to market value, is what a property actually sells for. Market price should theoretically be the same as market value if all the conditions essential for market value were present. Market price, however, may not reflect the analysis of comparables and of investment value that an estimate of market value includes.

APPRAISING OR ESTIMATING MARKET VALUE

An appraisal is distinguished from other estimates of value in that it is an opinion of value supported by data and performed by a professional, disinterested third party. Appraisers acting in a professional capacity are also regulated by state laws and bound to standards set by the appraisal industry.

The appraisal itself is used in real estate decision-making to estimate one or more types of value, depending on the kind of decision to be made. Appraisals may be ordered and used by mortgage lenders, government agencies, investors, utilities companies, and real estate buyers and sellers.

An appraisal helps in setting selling prices and rental rates, determining the level of insurance coverage, establishing investment values, and establishing the value of the real estate as collateral for a loan.

Appraisals may be developed and reported in a narrative format or on a prescribed form with attachments. The most commonly used form for residential appraisals is the "Uniform Residential Appraisal Report" (URAR) promoted by the Federal National Mortgage Association (FNMA) and Federal Home Loan Mortgage Corporation (FHLMC) (known as Fannie Mae and Freddie Mac, respectively).

Steps in the appraisal process

Define the problem. The first step in the process is to define the appraisal problem and the purpose of the appraisal. This involves

- identifying the subject property by legal description
- specifying the interest to be appraised
- specifying the purpose of the appraisal, for example, to identify market value for a purchase, identify rental levels, or establish a value as collateral for a loan
- specifying the date for which the appraisal is valid
- identifying the type of value to be estimated

Execute required steps. The remaining steps of the appraisal process are:

- assimilating relevant data – collecting, organizing, and analyzing relevant data about the subject property. Information relevant to the property includes notes and drawings from physical inspection of the subject, public tax and title records, and reproduction costs. Relevant information about the market includes environmental, demographic, and economic reports concerning the neighborhood, community, and region.
- assessing the highest and best use – analyzing market conditions to identify the most profitable use for the subject property. This use may or may not be the existing use.
- estimating the value of the land- an appraiser does this by comparing the subject site, but not its buildings, with similar sites in the area, and making adjustments for significant differences.
- applying the three approaches to estimating value-: *the sales comparison approach, the cost approach, and the income capitalization approach*. Using multiple methods serves to guard against errors and to set a range of values for the final estimate.
- reconciling the values from the approaches- reconciling the value estimates produced by the three approaches to value into a final value estimate.
- compiling the report- presenting the estimate of value in the format requested by the client.

VALUING RESIDENTIAL PROPERTY- THE MARKET DATA APPROACH

The sales comparison approach/ market data approach is a method of estimating value that relies on the principle that a property is generally worth what other, similar properties are worth.

The sales comparison approach, also known as the *market data approach*, is used for almost all properties. It also serves as the basis for a broker's opinion of value. It is based on the principle of substitution-- that a buyer will pay no more for the subject property than would be sufficient to purchase a comparable property-- and contribution-- that specific characteristics add value to a property.

The sales comparison approach is widely used because it takes into account the subject property's specific amenities in relation to competing properties. In addition, because of the currency of its data, the approach incorporates present market realities.

The sales comparison approach is limited in that every property is unique. As a result, it is difficult to find good comparables, especially for special-purpose properties. In addition, the market must be active; otherwise, sale prices lack currency and reliability.

Steps in the Sales Comparison Approach

The sales comparison approach consists of comparing sale prices of recently sold properties that are comparable with the subject and making dollar adjustments to the price of each comparable to account for competitive differences with the subject. After identifying the adjusted value of each comparable, the appraiser weights the reliability of each comparable and the factors underlying how the adjustments were made. The weighting yields a final value range based on the most reliable factors in the analysis.

1. Identify comparable sales.
2. Compare comparables to the subject and make adjustments to comparables.
3. Weight values indicated by adjusted comparables for the final value estimate of the subject.

Identifying comparables

To qualify as a comparable, a property must:

1. resemble the subject in size, shape, design, utility and location
2. have sold recently, generally within six months of the appraisal
3. have sold in an arm's-length transaction

Appraisers have specific guidelines within the foregoing criteria for selecting comparables, many of which are set by secondary market organizations such as FNMA. For example, to qualify as a comparable for a mortgage loan appraisal, a property might have to be located within one mile of the subject. Or perhaps the size of the comparable must be within a certain percentage of improved area in relation to the subject.

The time-of-sale criterion is important because transactions that occurred too far in the past will not reflect appreciation or recent changes in market conditions.

An arm's length sale involves objective, disinterested parties who are presumed to have negotiated a market price for the property. If the sale of a house occurred between a father and a daughter, for example, one might assume that the transaction did not reflect market value.

Principal sources of data for generating the sales comparison are tax records, title records, and the local multiple listing service.

Adjusting comparables

The appraiser adjusts the sale prices of the comparables to account for competitive differences with the subject property. Note that the sale prices of the comparables are known, while the value and price of the subject are not. Therefore, adjustments can be made *only to the comparables' prices, not to the subject's.* Adjustments are made to the comparables in the form of a value deduction or a value addition.

Adding or deducting value. If the comparable is *better* than the subject in some characteristic, an amount is *deducted* from the sale price of the comparable. This neutralizes the comparable's competitive advantage in an adjustment category.

For example, a comparable has a swimming pool and the subject does not. To equalize the difference, the appraiser deducts an amount, say $6,000, from the sale price of the comparable. Note that the adjustment reflects the contribution of the swimming pool to market value. The adjustment amount is not the cost of the pool or its depreciated value.

If the comparable is *inferior* to the subject in some characteristic, an amount is *added* to the price of the comparable. This adjustment equalizes the subject's competitive advantage in this area.

Adjustment criteria. The principal factors for comparison and adjustment are *time of sale, location, physical characteristics, and transaction characteristics.*

▸ **time of sale**

An adjustment may be made if market conditions, market prices, or financing availability have changed significantly since the date of the comparable's sale. Most often, this adjustment is to account for appreciation.

▸ **location**

An adjustment may be made if there are differences between the comparable's location and the subject's, including neighborhood desirability and appearance, zoning restrictions, and general price levels.

▸ **physical characteristics**

Adjustments may be made for marketable differences between the comparable's and subject's lot size, square feet of livable area (or other appropriate measure for the property type), number of rooms, layout, age, condition, construction type and quality, landscaping, and special amenities.

▸ **transaction characteristics**

An adjustment may be made for such differences as mortgage loan terms, mortgage assumability, and owner financing.

Weighting comparables

Adding and subtracting the appropriate adjustments to the sale price of each comparable results in an adjusted price for the comparables that indicates the value of the subject. The last step in the approach is to perform a weighted analysis of the indicated values of each comparable. The appraiser, in other words, must identify which comparable values are more indicative of the subject and which are less indicative.

An appraiser primarily relies on experience and judgment to weight comparables. There is no formula for selecting a value from within the range of all comparables analyzed. However, there are three quantitative guidelines: the total number of adjustments; the amount of a single adjustment; and the net value change of all adjustments.

As a rule, *the fewer the total number of adjustments, the smaller the adjustment amounts, and the less the total adjustment amount, the more reliable the comparable.*

Number of adjustments. In terms of total adjustments, the comparable with the fewest adjustments tends to be most similar to the subject, hence the best indicator of value. If a comparable requires excessive adjustments, it is increasingly less reliable as an indicator of value. The underlying rationale is that there is a margin of error involved in making any adjustment. Whenever a number of adjustments must be made, the margin of error compounds. By the time six or seven adjustments are made, the margin becomes significant, and the reliability of the final value estimate is greatly reduced.

Single adjustment amounts. The dollar amount of an adjustment represents the variance between the subject and the comparable for a given item. If a large adjustment is called for, the comparable becomes less of an indicator of value. The smaller the adjustment, the better the comparable is as an indicator of value. If an appraisal is performed for mortgage qualification, the appraiser may be restricted from making adjustments in excess of a certain amount, for example, anything in excess of 10-15% of the sale price of the comparable. If such an adjustment would be necessary, the property is no longer considered comparable.

Total net adjustment amount. The third reliability factor in weighting comparables is the total net value change of all adjustments added together. If a comparable's total adjustments alter the indicated value only slightly, the comparable is a good indicator of value. If total adjustments create a large dollar amount between the sale price and the adjusted value, the comparable is a poorer indicator of value. Fannie Mae, for instance, will not accept the use of a comparable where total net adjustments are in excess of 15% of the sale price.

For example, an appraiser is considering a property that sold for $100,000 as a comparable. After all adjustments are made, the indicated value of the comparable is $121,000, a 21% difference in the comparable's sale price. This property, if allowed at all, would be a weak indicator of value.

BROKER'S COMPARATIVE MARKET ANALYSIS (CMA)

A broker or salesperson who is attempting to establish a listing price or range of prices for a property uses a scaled-down version of the appraiser's sales comparison approach called a comparative market analysis, or CMA (also called a competitive market analysis). While the CMA serves a useful purpose in setting general price ranges, brokers and agents need to exercise caution in presenting a CMA as an appraisal, which it is not. Two important distinctions between the two are objectivity and comprehensiveness.

First, the broker is not unbiased: he or she is motivated by the desire to obtain a listing, which can lead one to distort the estimated price. Secondly, the broker's CMA is not comprehensive: the broker does not usually consider the full range of data about market conditions and comparable sales that the appraiser must consider and document. Therefore, the broker's opinion will be less reliable than the appraiser's.

THE INCOME CAPITALIZATION APPROACH

The income capitalization approach, or income approach, is used for income properties and sometimes for other properties in a rental market where the appraiser can find rental data. The approach is based on the principle of anticipation: the expected future income stream of a property underlies what an investor will pay for the property. It is also based on the principle of substitution: that an investor will pay no more for a subject property with a certain income stream than the investor would have to pay for another property with a similar income stream.

The strength of the income approach is that it is used by investors themselves to determine how much they should pay for a property. Thus, in the right circumstances, it provides a good basis for estimating market value.

The income capitalization approach is limited in two ways. First, it is difficult to determine an appropriate capitalization rate. This is often a matter of judgment and experience on the part of the appraiser. Secondly, the income approach relies on market information about income and expenses, and it can be difficult to find such information.

The income capitalization method consists of estimating annual net operating income from the subject property, then applying a capitalization rate to the income. This produces a principal amount that the investor would pay for the property.

Steps in the Income Capitalization Approach

1. Estimate potential gross income.

2. Estimate effective gross income.

3. Estimate net operating income.

4. Select a capitalization rate.

5. Apply the capitalization rate.

Estimate potential gross income. Potential gross income is the scheduled rent of the subject plus income from miscellaneous sources such as vending machines and telephones. Scheduled rent is the total rent a property will produce if fully leased at the established rental rates.

Scheduled rent and Other income

Potential gross income

An appraiser may estimate potential gross rental income using current market rental rates (market rent), the rent specified by leases in effect on the property (contract rent), or a combination of both. Market rent is determined by market studies in a process similar to the sales comparison method. Contract rent is used primarily if the existing leases are not due to expire in the short term and the tenants are unlikely to fail or leave the lease.

Estimate effective gross income. Effective gross income is potential gross income minus an allowance for vacancy and credit losses.

Potential gross income

- Vacancy & credit losses

Effective gross income

Vacancy loss refers to an amount of potential income lost because of unrented space. Credit loss refers to an amount lost because of tenants' failure to pay rent for any reason. Both are estimated on the basis of the subject property's history, comparable properties in the market, and assuming typical management quality. The allowance for vacancy and credit loss is usually estimated as a percentage of potential gross income.

Estimate net operating income. Net operating income is effective gross income minus total operating expenses:

Effective gross income - Total operating expenses = Net operating income

Operating expenses include fixed expenses and variable expenses. Fixed expenses are those that are incurred whether the property is occupied or vacant, for example, real estate taxes and hazard insurance. Variable expenses are those that relate to actual operation of the building, for example, utilities, janitorial service, management, and repairs.

Operating expenses typically include an annual reserve fund for replacement of equipment and other items that wear out periodically, such as carpets and heating systems. Operating expenses do not include debt service, expenditures for capital improvements, or expenses not related to operation of the property.

Select a capitalization rate. The capitalization rate is an estimate of the rate of return an investor will demand on the investment of capital in a property such as the subject. The judgment and market knowledge of the appraiser play an essential role in the selection of an appropriate rate for the subject property. In most cases, the appraiser will research capitalization rates used on similar properties in the market.

Apply the capitalization rate. An appraiser now obtains an indication of value from the income capitalization method by dividing the estimated net operating income for the subject by the selected capitalization rate

Using the traditional symbols for income (I), rate (R) and value (V), the formula for value is:

$$I / R = V$$

==

Income approach illustration

Data. A quadplex property currently has a gross rental income of $192,000 per year. On top of the rental income, there is also a laundromat on site that brings in $2,000/year. The units did not remain occupied all year and there were about $9,600 in vacancy and collection losses. In addition to the losses, the owner also incurred the following operating expenses: real estate taxes ($32,000), insurance costs ($4,400), utilities ($12,000), repairs for the units ($4,000), maintenance ($16,000), management costs ($12,000), reserves ($1,600), and legal and accounting fees ($2,000). Similar quadplexes in that area have a capitalization rate of 7%.

Analysis. What is the value using the income approach?

    I. ESTIMATE POTENTIAL GROSS INCOME

        Potential gross rental income   192,000

        Plus: other income   2,000

        Potential gross income 194,000

    II. ESTIMATE EFFECTIVE GROSS INCOME

        Less: vacancy and collection losses   9,600

        Effective gross income 184,400

    III. ESTIMATE NET OPERATING INCOME

        Operating expenses:

        Real estate taxes   32,000

        Insurance   4,400

        Utilities 12,000

        Repairs 4,000

        Maintenance   16,000

        Management   12,000

Reserves   1,600

Legal and accounting   2,000

Total operating expenses   84,000

Effective gross income 184,400

Less: total expenses   84,000

Net operating income   100,400

IV. SELECT CAPITALIZATION RATE

Capitalization rate: 7%

V. APPLY CAPITALIZATION RATE: **I/R = V**

100,400 / .07   = $1,434,300 (rounded)

Indicated value by income approach: 1,434,300

Income approach conclusion. The first step in determining value using the income approach was to estimate the potential gross income. This was the combined income from the rent and the laundromat and totaled to $194,000. Next, the effective gross income had to be calculated which was the result of subtracting the vacancy and credit losses ($9,600) from the potential gross income ($194,000). The effective gross income resulted in $184,400. The third step was to estimate the net operating income. Before jumping into that, the total operating expenses had to be calculated which added up to $84,000. This amount was then subtracted from the effective gross income to yield a net operating income of $100,400. Using the common capitalization rate of 7% the value was determined by dividing the net operating income by the capitalization rate. The value was then found to be $1,434,300

Check Your Understanding Challenges:

Chapter Five: Estimating Market Value

Carefully read each question then provide your best answer based on what you learned in this chapter. Then check your answers against the Answer Key which immediately follows the chapter questions.

1. The concept of market value in true appraising terms implies a number of conditions have been met to authenticate the ending value estimate. One such condition is that the parties cannot be related because this could distort what two disinterested parties might pay. The text lists six other conditions. Can you name four of these?

       1._____

       2._____

       3,_____

       4._____

2. Which appraisal approach serves as the basis for a broker's opinion of value?

    _____

    _____

3. Identify the three steps in the Sales Comparison Approach:

      1.   _____

      2.   _____

      3.   _____

4. In a CMA, comparables must be adjusted to make them quantitatively equivalent to the subject property. One such adjustment is location factors. What are the three other major categories of adjustment?

    _____

    _____

    _____

5. If the comparable is *better* than the subject in some characteristic, an amount is *deducted* from the sale price of the comparable. True or false?

6. An appraiser is considering a property that sold for $100,000 as a comparable. After all adjustments are made, the indicated value of the comparable is $130,000, a 30% difference in the comparable's sale price. This property, if allowed at all, this comparable would be a

    a. weak indicator of value.

    b. strong indicator of value.

    c. perfect indicator of value.

    d. likely indicator of value.

7. Identify the steps in the Income Capitalization Approach:

    1. _____

    2. _____

    3. _____

    4. _____

    5. _____

    6. _____

Answer Key: Check Your Understanding Challenges

Chapter Five: Estimating Market Value

1. The concept of market value in true appraising terms implies a number of conditions have been met to authenticate the ending value estimate. One such condition is that the parties cannot be related because this could distort what two disinterested parties might pay. The text lists six other conditions. Can you name four of these?

> **transaction is for cash**
>
> **property is exposed to the market for a reasonable period**
>
> **buyer and seller are reasonably informed about market conditions and potential uses**
>
> **there is no coercion or abnormal pressure applied to principals**
>
> **title is marketable**
>
> **price involves conventional consideration – no secret concessions**

2. Which appraisal approach serves as the basis for a broker's opinion of value?

> **The sales comparison approach, also known as the *market data approach*, serves as the basis for a broker's opinion of value.**

3. Identify the three steps in the Sales Comparison Approach:

> **1. Identify comparable sales.**
> **2. Compare comparables to the subject and make adjustments to comparables.**
> **3. Weight values indicated by adjusted comparables for the final value estimate of the subject**

4. What are the major categories of adjustment?

> **1. Location**
> **2. time of sale**
> **3. physical characteristics**
> **4. transaction characteristics**

5. If the comparable is *better* than the subject in some characteristic, an amount is *deducted* from the value of the comparable. **True**

> **If the comparable is better than the subject, deduct value from the comparable. If the comparable is worse than the subject, add value to the comparable. Never adjust the subject!**

6. An appraiser is considering a property that sold for $100,000 as a comparable. After all adjustments are made, the indicated value of the comparable is $130,000, a 30% difference in the comparable's sale price. This property, if allowed at all, this comparable would be a

> **a. weak indicator of value**.

Total adjustments to a comparable should not exceed 15%. Otherwise there is too much dissimilarity between the comparable and the subject, and therefore the comp is not a very reliable indicator of value.

7. Identify the steps in the Income Capitalization Approach:

1. **Estimate potential gross income.**
2. **Estimate effective gross income.**
3. **Estimate net operating income.**
4. **Select a capitalization rate.**
5. **Apply the capitalization rate.**

==

Interactive Exercises

Chapter 5: Estimating Market Value

DEMONSTRATION EXAMPLE 3: Completing a Comparative Market Analysis (CMA)

Read the case scenario then complete the following worksheet to determine the CMA's price estimate. Note the worksheet has "equal" already entered where no adjustment is called for ant a "$_____" where an adjustment is called for. Be sure to include a "+" or a "-" to signify a positive or negative adjustment.

Assumed adjustment amounts:

Location: $20,000	*# Bedrooms: $10,000 per room*
Age: $20,000	*# Bathrooms: $10,000 per room*
Lot size: $10,000	*Gross living area: $10,000 per 100 feet*
Condition: $20,000	

Deandra is preparing for her listing appointment next week and in order to determine an appropriate price for the home she runs a comparative market analysis (CMA).

Here is the data for the subject property and comparables.

Subject:

8 rooms-- 3 bedrooms, two baths, kitchen, living room, family room; 2,500 square feet of gross living area; **3-car** attached garage; condition is good. Construction is wood frame with aluminum siding.

Comparable A:

Sold for $850,000; located in subject's neighborhood with similar locational advantages; house approximately same age as subject; lot size similar to subject; condition similar to subject; two bedrooms, one bath; 2,200 square feet of gross living area.

Comparable B:

Sold for $950,000; located in subject's neighborhood with similar locational advantages; house ten years newer than subject; lot size considerably larger than the subject's; better condition than subject; four bedrooms, three baths; gross living area is similar.

Comparable C:

Sold for $1,000,000; located in subject's neighborhood with similar locational advantages; house eight years older than subject; lot size similar to subject; condition similar to subject; three bedrooms, three baths; 2,500 square feet of gross living area.

Comparable D:

Sold for 1,090,000; located in a more desirable neighborhood than subject; house approximately same age and size and condition as subject, with two bedrooms, and two baths; 1,900 square feet of gross living area.

Please use the foregoing information to fill out the CMA table below. An "equal" evaluation has been entered where no adjustments are necessary.

CMA Adjustment table

	Subject	A	B	C	D
Sale price	???	850,000	950,000	1,000,000	1,090,000
Location		equal	equal	equal	$_____
Age		equal	$_____	$_____	equal
Lot size		equal	$_____	equal	equal
Condition		equal	$_____	equal	equal
No. of bedrooms	3	$_____	$_____	equal	$_____
No. of baths	2	$_____	$_____	$_____	equal
Gross living area	2,500	$_____	equal	equal	$_____
Net adjustments					
Indicated value					

Case Debrief:

Sales Comparison Approach

Adjustments

	Subject	A	B	C	D
Sale price		850,000	950,000	1,000,000	1,090,000
Location		equal	equal	equal	-20,000
Age		equal	-20,000	+20,000	equal
Lot size		equal	-10,000	equal	equal
Condition	good	equal	-20,000	equal	equal
No. of bedrooms	3	+10,000	-10,000	equal	+10,000
No. of baths	2	+10,000	-10,000	equal	equal
Gross living area	2,500	+30,000	equal	equal	+60,000
Net adjustments		+50,000	-70,000	+20,000	+50,000
Indicated value	1,000,000	900,000	880,000	1,020,000	1,140,000

For comparable A, the appraiser has made additions, number of bedrooms and baths, and for gross living area. A total of three adjustments amount to $50,000, or 4.8% of the purchase price.

For comparable B, the appraiser has deducted values for age, lot, condition, bedrooms, and baths. A total of five adjustments amount to $70,000, or 8% of the sale price.

For comparable C, the appraiser has adjusted for the age. The adjustments total 20,000 raising the indicated value of the subject to $1,020,000.

For comparable D, a deduction has been made for the comparable's superior location. This is offset by the number of bedrooms and gross living area additions reflecting where the comparable is inferior to the subject. A total of three adjustments amount to +$50,000, or 4.6% of the sale price.

Conclusion. In view of all adjusted comparables, the appraiser developed a final indication of value of $1,000,000 for the subject. Underlying this conclusion is the fact that Comparable C is by far the best indicator of value. Comparable D might be the second-best indicator, since the net adjustments are very close to the sale price. Comparable A might be the third best indicator, since it has the second fewest number of total adjustments. Comparable B is the least reliable indicator, since there are numerous adjustments.

CHAPTER 6:

OTHER LAWS & REGULATIONS AFFECTING BROKERAGE FUNCTIONS

Chapter Six Learning Objectives: When the student has completed this chapter he or she will be able to:

- Define broker cooperation and describe generally how cooperation works in the context of the multiple listing services.
- Define 'teams' and highlight several areas of concern with teams that have become regulated..
- Identify forms of compensation and summarize the principal regulations surrounding compensation and how and when it can be legitimately received
- Summarize the principal regulations framing compliant real estate advertising practice, including identifications; web advertising; electronic communications and prohibitions
- Identify what activities unlicensed assistants can legally undertake
- Summarize what brokerage activities constitute 'licensed activities' requiring an active real estate license

BROKER COOPERATION

The core activity of real estate brokerage is the business of procuring a buyer, seller, tenant, or property on behalf of a client for the purpose of completing a transaction. If successful, the broker receives a commission according to the provisions of a listing agreement. A broker's compensation for effecting a transaction is usually a negotiated percentage of the purchase price.

Broker cooperation. In most cases, transactions require the assistance of a cooperating broker from another brokerage company acting as a subagent. Most listing agreements provide for brokerage cooperation in the multiple listing clause. A transaction involving a cooperating subagent is called co-brokerage. In a co-brokered transaction, the listing broker splits the commission with the "co-broker." A broker may cooperate with other brokers on either side of a transaction, either assisting a listing agent to locate a buyer or tenant, or assisting a buyer or tenant representative in locating a seller or landlord.

In the most common form of broker cooperation, an outside broker locates a buyer for the listing broker's seller. In such cases, the listing broker shares the commission with the cooperating "selling" broker on a pre-determined basis.

TEAMS

It is not uncommon for licensees to function as part of a real estate team. It is the designated managing broker's responsibility to ensure that the team operates in compliance with agency, advertising, and other applicable laws. The company policy may dictate whether teams acts as dual agents, and if not, what procedures must be taken to ensure client confidentiality within the team.

Team advertising can be a problem if the team has a team name. The designated managing broker must ensure that the sponsoring brokerage name appears in team ads, and that the team name does not mislead or give the public the impression that it is a separate company. Teams may not operate under an assumed business name other than that of the sponsoring broker.

COMMISSIONS AND COMPENSATION

Compensation includes:

- commissions, referral fees, bonuses
- prizes and merchandise
- finder fees
- performance of services
- coupons or gift certificates
- discounts or rebates
- chance to win a raffle, drawing, lottery, or similar game of chance not prohibited by any other law or statute
- retainer fee
- salary

Commissions generally are considered earned when the broker accomplishes the contracted task (i.e., has obtained an accepted offer). The commission is considered payable at closing, as closing is proof of the commission being earned. To collect a commission, an individual must be licensed and have an employment agreement (i.e., listing or buyer agency agreement).

A sponsoring broker may collect compensation without being procuring cause if he or she has a contract with a client that provides for collection (i.e. an exclusive listing or buyer agency agreement). Procuring cause is a National Association of REALTORS® requirement in connection with an MLS offer of cooperation.

Compensation is paid to the sponsoring broker, based on the brokerage agreement with the client, at or shortly after closing the transaction, based on practices in each area.

Commissions and other fees for real estate activity can be paid only to sponsoring brokers. The sponsoring broker may then share the compensation with sponsored licensees involved in the transaction, based on the written agreement with the licensee. Sponsoring brokers may not pay compensation to licensees sponsored by another broker.

Sponsoring brokers may share compensation with cooperating sponsoring brokers in Illinois and other locations, with licensees no longer affiliated with the broker but who were licensed with the broker at the time the commission was earned, and with Illinois auctioneers who are real estate certified.

Sponsored licensees may be paid only by the sponsoring broker with whom they are contracted. Licensees may not be paid by other sponsoring brokers, other licensees, or consumers. Sponsored licensees may share compensation with a principal to a transaction.

The sponsoring broker may pay compensation directly to an entity owned solely by a licensee and formed to receive compensation earned by the licensee. An entity formed for this reason may only receive compensation earned by the licensee. The entity must be owned solely by the licensee, or by the licensee together with the licensee's spouse, but only if the spouse and licensee are both licensed and sponsored by the same sponsoring broker or the spouse is not licensed. The entity is not required to be licensed (Sec. 1450.745).

ADVERTISING REGULATION

All advertising must be carried out in the name of the sponsoring broker.

Advertising includes print, electronic, social media and digital forums (225 ILCS 45, Sect. 10).

Prohibitions

Deceptive or misleading advertising is prohibited, and includes:

- advertising property exclusively listed with another sponsoring broker without permission and identification of the listing broker
- failing to remove property ads within a reasonable time of closing or termination of the listing agreement, whichever occurs first
- advertising property at an auction as an absolute auction when it is not
- advertising in a way that creates confusion regarding the permitted use of the property, such as "apartment", "separate living arrangement" or similar wording, unless the use is permitted by zoning law
- advertising in a way that does not display the sponsoring broker's name or assumed name in a reasonably apparent manner
- failing to display the broker's business name in a size at least equal to or larger than that of the name of the team or individual licensee (225 ILCS 454 Sect. 10-30(f)
- using misleading terms for teams, such as "company," "realty," "real estate," "agency," "associates," "brokers," "properties," or "property" (225 ILCS 454, Sect. 10-30)
- advertising in a manner that is fraudulent, misleading, deceptive or misleading in practice; it is considered misleading or untruthful if, when taken as a whole, there is a distinct and reasonable possibility that it will be misunderstood or will deceive

Internet advertising

Licensees must include their licensing information, along with the licensee's name as licensed and the city and state of the licensee's office. If the information is on the frame of a web page, it does not need to be included on every page.

To advertise a property listed exclusively with another sponsoring broker, a broker advertising the property on the Internet must obtain written permission from, and identify in the ad, the listing sponsoring broker.

Licensees must periodically review and update advertising information on websites to ensure the information is current and not misleading.

E-commerce and electronic communications

A sponsoring broker must include on all communication the sponsoring broker's name as licensed, and the city and state where the sponsoring broker's office is located. Other licensees must also include the information, plus the licensee's name as licensed. This does not apply if a member of the public sent a communication and the initial communication contained the information.

Licensees intending to sell or share consumer information gained from or through the Internet or other electronic means must disclose that intention to consumers in a timely and apparent manner.

Linking to other websites

A licensee may link to listing information from another brokerage's website or from a multiple listing service without express approval unless the website owner specifically requires consent. Links must not mislead or deceive the public regarding ownership of any listing information.

Licensees may not engage in phishing (using email or other electronic communication to obtain personal or sensitive information by disguising the real sender). Using a URL, domain name, metatag, or keyword to divert or direct internet traffic or to deceive or mislead is prohibited. Licensees are also prohibited from framing another brokerage or multiple listing service website deceptively or without required authorization (225 ILCS 454, Sect. 10).

LICENSE STATUS DISCLOSURE

Licensed managing brokers who are so designated by their sponsoring brokers must identify themselves as designated managing brokers in advertising other than for sale or similar signage. Licensed managing brokers not so designated may use the term "managing broker" but may not use "designated managing broker" (225 ILCS 454, Sect. 10-30).

The same applies to the use of e-mail, e-mail discussion groups and e-bulletin boards for marketing.

UNLICENSED EMPLOYEES

Licensees may use unlicensed individuals to assist with non-licensed activities. Compensation for unlicensed individuals cannot be based on transactions. A licensee supervising an unlicensed individual is responsible for that person's actions.

It is unlawful for any unlicensed person to advertise or act as a licensee without a license issued by the Department.

Real estate assistant or personal assistant

Brokers may hire licensed or unlicensed employees to assist them with a variety of tasks. Unlicensed assistants may perform clerical or ministerial acts, but nothing requiring a license. Licensed assistants may perform tasks requiring a license. Unlicensed assistants usually may be compensated directly by the broker they work for, but licensed assistants must be compensated by the employing broker and are subject to that broker's supervision.

LICENSED ACTIVITIES

Any person who performs licensed acts must first obtain a broker or managing broker license. The Act defines persons as individuals, entities, corporations, limited liability companies, registered limited liability partnerships, and partnerships, foreign or domestic. Businesses wishing to conduct real estate activities are required to first obtain a broker license.

Licensed activities are included in the definition of broker. A license is required if these duties are performed for another and for compensation, or with the intention of receiving compensation, whether the duties are performed personally or through media or technology.

Specific licensed activities. Performing or attempting to perform any of the following activities without first obtaining a license is a violation of the Act and can result in disciplinary action by the Department:

- selling, exchanging, purchasing, renting, or leasing real estate, or offering or negotiating these activities
- listing real estate, or offering or attempting to list it; includes listing for sale, rent, lease, or exchange
- whether for another or themselves, engaging in a pattern of business of buying, selling, or offering to buy or sell, marketing for sale, exchanging, or otherwise dealing in contracts for the purchase or sale of, or options on, real estate improvements; an individual or entity will be found to have engaged in a pattern of business if, by itself or with any combination of other individuals or entities, whether as partners or common owners in another entity, it has engaged in one or more of these practices on two or more occasions in any 12-month period
- supervising the collection of or agreeing to collect rent
- advertising or representing that one is engaged in real estate activities
- assisting in procuring or referring leads or prospects for the sale, exchange, lease or rental of real estate
- assisting or directing the negotiation of a transaction intended to result in the sale, exchange, lease or rental of real
- opening real estate to the public for marketing purposes; a non-licensee may not host open houses, kiosks, or home show booths
- selling, renting, leasing or offering real estate for sale at an auction
- preparing or providing a broker price opinion or comparative market analysis
- receiving compensation for licensed activities or receiving anything of value for a referral of real estate business

Compensating non-licensees. A licensee may not pay, or give anything of value, to an unlicensed person who provides names of potential clients. A neighbor who provides a licensee with the name of a potential buyer or seller cannot be paid or otherwise compensated by the licensee, unless the neighbor is a real estate licensee and is paid through the sponsoring broker.

Practicing without a license. Practicing without a license can result in a civil penalty of up to $25,000 for each offense, assessed by the Department after a hearing. The penalty becomes a judgment. The Department has the authority to investigate any unlicensed activity. Any unlicensed person found guilty of performing licensed activity or representing that he or she is a licensee is guilty of a Class A misdemeanor, and a second or subsequent offense is a Class 4 felony (Sec. 20-22). No applicant may engage in any licensed activities without a valid license and until a valid sponsorship has been registered with the Department

==

Check Your Understanding Challenges:

Chapter Six: Other Laws & Regulations Affecting Brokerage Functions

Carefully read each question then provide your best answer based on what you learned in this chapter. Then check your answers against the Answer Key which immediately follows the chapter questions.

1. It is the _____ responsibility to ensure that the team operates in compliance with agency, advertising, and other applicable laws. Fill in the blank with your answer.

   A. Team leader's
   B. Team member's
   C. Sponsored licensee's
   D. Designated managing broker's

2. The sponsoring brokerage name must always appear in team ads. True or false?

3. Teams may operate under an assumed business name other than that of the sponsoring broker. True or false?

4. As a licensee your accountant has advised you to consider setting up a corporation for the purpose of receiving compensation. In this case, the sponsoring broker may pay compensation directly to your entity if

   a. The entity is owned solely by you.
   b. The entity was formed to receive compensation earned by your team.
   c. The entity is also owned by your spouse who is sponsored by a broker in a neighboring town.
   d. The entity is licensed.

5. Which of the following qualifies as misleading advertising?

   a. Advertising property exclusively listed with another sponsoring broker with their permission.
   b. Removing property ads 24 hours after the day of the closing.
   c. Placing advertising that does not display the sponsoring broker's name.
   d. Displaying the broker's business name in a size larger than that of the name of the team.

6. Checkmark all TRUE statements:

1. Licensees may use unlicensed individuals to assist with non-licensed activities.
2. Licensees may use unlicensed individuals to assist with licensed activities providing that they are supervised.
3. Compensation for unlicensed individuals cannot be based on transactions.
4. Unlicensed individuals cannot be compensated.
5. A licensee supervising an unlicensed individual is responsible for that person's actions.
6. It is not unlawful for any unlicensed person to advertise.
7. It is unlawful for any unlicensed person to act as a licensee without a license issued by the Department.

Answer Key: Check Your Understanding Challenges

Chapter Six: Other Laws & Regulations Affecting Brokerage Functions

1. It is the _____ responsibility to ensure that the team operates in compliance with agency, advertising, and other applicable laws. FILL IN THE BLANK

   d. Designated managing broker's

2. The sponsoring brokerage name must always appear in team ads.

   True

3. Teams may operate under an assumed business name other than that of the sponsoring broker.

   False

4. As a licensee your accountant has advised you to consider setting up a corporation for the purpose of receiving compensation. In this case, the sponsoring broker may pay compensation directly to your entity if

   a. The entity is owned solely by you.

5. Which of the following qualifies as misleading advertising?

   c. Placing advertising that does not display the sponsoring broker's name.

6. All true statements are in bold:

   1. **Licensees may use unlicensed individuals to assist with non-licensed activities.**
   2. Licensees may use unlicensed individuals to assist with licensed activities providing that they are supervised.
   3. **Compensation for unlicensed individuals cannot be based on transactions.**
   4. Unlicensed individuals cannot be compensated.
   5. **A licensee supervising an unlicensed individual is responsible for that person's actions.**
   6. **It is not unlawful for any unlicensed person to advertise.**
   7. **It is unlawful for any unlicensed person to act as a licensee without a license issued by the Department.**

===

Interactive Exercises

Chapter 6: Other Laws Affecting Brokerage Functions

ROLE PLAY / SITUATIONAL CASE STUDY 7: Managing assistants

Taylor is in her fifth year of business and is feeling overwhelmed with booking showings, administrative work, negotiating contracts, and everything else that being a real estate agent entails. She is hoping to hire an assistant but does not know where to start so she posts about it on an online job board. After interviewing a few candidates she finally lands on Austin who seems like he will be the best fit. She only needs him to work 10-15 hours a week hosting open houses, booking showings, and acting as a transaction coordinator once her deals are under contract. He meets all of her criteria- he's friendly, hard working, and has great job references.

What else should Taylor ask Austin before hiring him?

_____

_____

_____

_____

_____

_____

_____

_____

_____

_____

Taylor needs to clarify whether Austin is a licensed real estate agent. He cannot participate in any activities that require a license- such as hosting open houses. He can only engage in clerical work that does not require a license if he's unlicensed.

Her job description should require the interviewees to have a license in order to prevent any future complications.

Made in the USA
Monee, IL
17 November 2022

17999972R00063